# Thoughts for a Better Tomorrow

# Thoughts for a Better Tomorrow

R. Jayaraman

Published by Zorba Books, May 2024
Website: www.zorbabooks.com
Email: info@zorbabooks.com
Author Name: R. Jayaraman


Title: Thoughts for a Better Tomorrow

Printbook ISBN: 978-93-5896-943-6
Ebook ISBN: 978-93-5896-374-8



**Zorba Books Pvt. Ltd. (opc)**
Sushant Arcade,
Next to Courtyard Marriot,
Sushant Lok 1, Gurgaon – 122009, India

Printed by Manipal Technologies Limited
A1 & A2 Shivalli Industrial Area Manipal Udupi, Karnataka – 57610

# Contents

# Foreword

One may wonder why a book on blogs and thought leadership needs an introduction at all. True and valid. Like everything else, a subject has to be placed in a context. Discussing spirituality during a boxing match, asking for *kheer* at the Calypso Bar and Spirits Place, wanting to score a run in a football match, Could all be legitimate activities, but in the wrong setting, the wrong context. The context must be set, for something special to hold the attention of the reader. And so are the contents of this book.

Blogs have yet to come of age, although many are making valiant attempts to take it to the 'next level', whatever that may mean. Bloggers have been making serious efforts to garner the attention of the discernati amongst us, to be paid due attention as another source of profound thoughts, as a means of contributing to the general knowledge of the society. Notwithstanding the competition, which is truly monstrous- FB, Twitter, WhatsApp, LinkedIn, LinkedOut, emails, what have you – blogs have sprung up on the unsuspecting from various sources. Nowadays, one can see blogs in newspapers, websites, FB and all the other social cuckoos, fighting to grab eyeballs and raised eyebrows.

That the learned professors in the SPJIMR decided to take the plunge was an act of courage. Many of us have not had the opportunity to put our thoughts to the populace, some of us have even gone so far as to keep away from it. Yet, making a beginning was not very difficult. And what a start it has been. Subjects as distant as sports and academics, as esoteric as agony aunts and driverless cars, as diverse as economics and management, have not been spared the pen. The learning was quick and thoughts were put on paper before one could say Timbuktu. The literati that read and commented on these blogs are another important dimension. After all, where would the Big B and Rajnikanth be without their fans?

In the ensuing pages you will find yourself absorbed and lost, hopefully, in contemplation about what life can mean to a bunch of professors in a B School. Welcome to the world of thoughts, leadership and blogs.

– R. Jayaraman
Mumbai

# Chapter 1

# The Importance of Academics

**The three boxes approach and its applicability to lean thinking**

The three boxes approach is all about changing while continuing with 'business as usual'. It is like changing the trouser for a dhoti while wearing a shirt and socks. Dr. Vijay Govindarajan has built a construct which is, while being simple, is also eminently applicable to corporate life. Perhaps it is applicable in other parts of life too.

Take, for example, the political field, which is everyone's favourite whipping boy in India. People were fed up of the scam raj, so they brought in the new raj. Now this new raj is evolving. Things like MNREGA, GST, Aadhaar, all relics of the past have not only been continued but strengthened with some imaginative interlinking. However new initiatives like the curbing of the black money menace, introducing new tech in the railways, changing the power sector structure have all been taken up. Kill corruption, kill scams, kill opacity in transactions. This is classic three box.

Bring in the new through the latest tech – tweeting for direct contact with the masses bypassing the media (creating a new media, some might say), rocketing through ISRO (from WASRO this organisation has been brought into prominence by the PM's comments on the inexpensive Mars mission, to become ISRO. I am sure it will become WILLRO very soon, the way it is launching missiles of all shapes, sizes and technologies), online auctions, online filing of IT etc.

The methodology being adopted to bring about change in the Indian continent is clearly in line with the three boxes methodology. While the results of such actions are clear the leading indicators which have led to such massive changes are to be studied. For example, did the PM follow the Kotterian formula for creating the massive changes that have been achieved in such a short time? Take the case of the 'coalition for change'. This has clearly not happened. Only one person wanted the change – Narendra Modi. Neither Advani, nor MMJ nor Govindacharya ever spoke about such changes even when they were in power. In the case of the PM, he is the one-man team. However, he has been successful because he has found able lieutenants in Rajnath Singh, Jaitley, Venkaiah Naidu, Nirmala Seetharaman, Sushma Swaraj, Piyush Goel, Smriti Irani and Javadekar (and others too). All this has been possible only because of the karishma of the PM. The other pillar of the Kotter philosophy for transformational change is the agenda. In the incumbent case, the agenda was actually set by the previous government. So, the key lead indicators show that the movement has been well planned and under able execution, and should succeed, given time and participation.

Applying the three boxes approach to the subject of lean thinking, there are clear parallels. Lean thinking typically involves 'kaikaku' – drastic change. It also uses 'Kaizens", continuous incremental change under the PDCA umbrella. Also involved is the 'Gemba' which is merely to say 'go, see for yourself' and don't be guided only by your underlings. In fact, the Toyota slogan for lean is: 'Safety first, quality must, kaizen for ever'. It is said that for lean to take roots and flourish one must get rid of the 'foot draggers'. Just like what Jim Collins says in his book 'Good to Great' – get the right people on the bus. Further, it is not correct to say people are the assets in a company, the right people are.

For lean thinking actions one must take leave of the classical way of thinking – which is, cost is king. The new way is: customer is king, and the 'tail can, and does, wag the dog', or at least, majorly helps the dog. This is just a way of saying that the supply chain at the upstream end is a key driver in a company's efforts to serve customers. And, if the cost a little high to serve customers, to build loyalty, then so be it.

To conclude, the area of 'kaikaku' clearly belongs to Brahma (Taichi Ohno is a Toyota Brahma), keeping the right people and the right assets, as well as the right customers and serving them better belongs to Vishnu, while killing off old technology, removing assets which are not useful anymore and getting rid of foot draggers are where Shiva will be active. The level 5 leaders that Jim Collins talks about are the combo of Vishnu and Shiva, while the corporate board of directors is the Brahma. I am sure we will see more boxes in many more spheres of life. After all, once the trinity is involved, omnipresence, omnipotence and omniscience are not far behind.

## MBA education in India – what is in store for the future (PART I)

As they say, MBA education is as old as the newly formed hills, comparatively speaking. The origins of the MBA education can be traced back to the USA, with the Wharton school being the pioneer, starting off in 1881 followed by the illustrious Tuck School at Dartmouth and the one and only Harvard Business School. Much course work has flown down Boston colleges after the MBA education was kicked off. However, the reason why an MBA school started off in 1881 – some 40 years before Henry Ford invented his assembly line – and when industry was very much in its infancy is a mystery. Where was the need for such a degree, if there were no industries that would employ them? Or where were the large companies to employ them at that time, since Henry Ford came in much later? So, one is left with an impression that the MBA was an evolutionary matter, much like how engineering education began. The chicken and egg story all over.

With advance of time the MBA education produced some of the stalwarts of the industries which dotted the landscape. In modern times we have names like Shikha Sharma, Ravi Venkatesan, Cyrus Mistry, Raghavendra Rao, Ashank Desai from India who are all business leaders of the highest calibre and who have accomplished much after their education in management. According to the 'Educational Statistics at a Glance' published by the MHRD, in 2012-13 a little more than 22 % of post graduates (MBA and Ph D) of the total enrolled candidates were in management studies, while the same is only 2 % at the undergraduate level. And this doesn't include data on part timers, distance education enrollers and other certificate courses. Clearly management education is highly valued in India.

Management graduates from good schools get the highest paying jobs in all countries. Not only do they start off better but also do better over the employment life cycle. All these facts bear witness why this education gets a lot of media attention. Annual B School ranking is an important event at many leading business and general magazines. Most enrollers seek out the highest-ranking schools. And they leave lower ranked schools in favour of the higher ones even after paying the fees. Management education is horizontally and vertically competitive. Horizontally – in the course contents, in the setting of curricula, in pedagogic methods. Vertically – offering the best infrastructure, the best accommodation (compared with the IIM hostel rooms the IIT rooms have to eat humble pie, to put it politely), the best placement services, the best jobs. Fees are hitting the roof, by Indian standards. The fee-gap between management and non-management education has been increasing for the last many years, and one hopes that management education doesn't price itself out of the reckoning. Many foreign B schools say that have reached the limits of 'diseconomies of scale' and admissions are constantly threatened. Not only that, the management education system is acquiring a reputation of becoming elitist and meant only for those who can afford the high fees. This needs to change.

In this change the one thing that is at the heart of the matter is the contents and methodology of management education. Being a creature of the environment and having no anchor in any stream of knowledge, very unlike the sciences, the arts, commerce which are all stream based and well founded and anchored in their respective vocational or knowledge spheres, MBA education has been the favourite whipping boy of academics and non-academics alike. Everyone has a view on it, what it should include and not, how should it be taught and so on. There are as many proponents of the 'quant' school as there are those who oppose. The 'diversity brigade' accuse the 'quant quadrangle' of having usurped the MBA education from the 'Aam Aadmis' of arts, science and commerce background. Engineers seem to dominate MBA college admissions and they have set up the paraphernalia – exams, aptitude tests, psycho tests, the works – all in their mould, with a critical quant bias. No wonder there is some resistance building up.

Add to that the recent complexities of business itself. From retail, to IT, to IOT, to digital, to Industry 4.0, changes in the MBA environment are endemic. How do educators cope with this? There are three main forces impacting. Firstly, students' attention span is reducing, with the advent of social media, instant 'like' and 'thumbs down", mobile android phones, fast paced life, shorter tenures at jobs, lack of 'meaty' jobs (because consultancies do not have the big jobs, and consulting is the growing job sector for MBA's in India).

I have a feeling that this blog is getting too long. So, I will sign off now and put the rest of the stuff in PART II.

## MBA education in India – what is in store for the future (PART II)

Taking up from where we left off, (see 'MBA Education in India – what is in store for the future (PART I)' by the same author)

There are three main forces impacting. Firstly, students' attention span is reducing, with the advent of social media, instant 'like' and 'thumbs down", mobile android phones, fast paced life, shorter tenures at jobs, lack of 'meaty' jobs (because consultancies do not have the big jobs, and consulting is the growing job sector for MBA's in India). Second, the syllabus is constantly evolving. Topics come in and go out like a metronome. This is primarily because the needs of the industry are changing. Keeping pace with the drumbeat of the industry is a task which needs constant attention and quick response. Else there is a good chance of the B School becoming irrelevant. Third, the pedagogical methods are evolving, albeit more slowly than the syllabi. MOOC's, Blended Learning (SPJIMR has made a beginning in this), on-line MBA are some of the brand extensions where B Schools are treading fresh ground.

Of late one has been hearing of the 'burden' that MBA students have to carry. Too much of work, too many courses, too many assignments, too much of MBA! One is reminded of the periodical reports in the popular media on the burden that school students have to carry – their outsize, loaded (overloaded?) bags. These are just peripheral to learning and can get demonised, well beyond their 'ill effects'. For example, school students in India have to study three languages, history, geography, science, civics et al. In all, every day there are typically eight periods in which different subjects are taught. Each subject has a text and a notebook in which students make notes (hopefully). So that makes for at least 10 to 15 100 pages books to be carried. Plus, the compass box, scales, pens and pencils. If that is a burden then education is one too.

In the same vein MBA students, by definition, have to learn several streams of knowledge. All this has to be done in one year, so that, in the second year, they could study some of their specialisation subjects in depth. Thus, the MBA education in India tries to walk a tightrope between a general education and a specialised one. Perhaps the objective is to create general specialists!

However, that be, in this objective, one can easily see that courses vie with each other for the student's time and lead to a heavy pressure on everyday life. It should be the objective of the B School how to enable the students to deal with this pressure. One way could be to reduce the load, perhaps, the easy way, and the other is the Harvard way, to hope that students will dedicate themselves to studies. The argument of 'lack of time for reflection' and, another companion concept, 'doing live projects' should be seen in context and perspective.

In a student's life, the first 16 years are spent in studies, and the balance in a job (s). When in the education system, the student's primary job is to gain knowledge – and not worry about how to apply. Applying this knowledge, experiential learning will happen on the job(s) over the next 30 to 40 years. Thus, students in B Schools should be relieved of the constant battering that they will have to be 'employment ready'. This could de-stress them and allow them to spend more time to learn and handle the load with full concentration.

## Feedback and its place in academics

When I was thinking about topics on which to blog one stood out like a sore thumb, or as a pandora's box. Depends on which way you are looking at it. But look at it, one must. It will not go away, it will not lose its bite, it will not lose its relevance, its ability to make the world a better place.

Continuing on the 'depends' (one has been told that depends is a defensive word, but on the other hand, of what use is an economist with only one hand?) idea let us see the various facets of this phenomenon which has been praised by Bill Gates as an activity, without which, American teachers are missing a great opportunity to improve oneself. Fair enough, after all, one has to listen to Gates as he opened the gates for wealth to thousands of Microsofters, of whom many have gone on to become Hardcurrencers!

Feedback is a process, the intention of which is to provide opportunities. I think this is culture specific. If we turn to Indian stories, there is no mention of how Lord Rama gave feedback to the great sage Vishwamitra under whose tutelage he learnt the three R's and many other things. How did the great archer Arjuna give feedback to Dronacharya from whom he learnt the art and science of aiming and hitting the object.

How we wish that both Valmiki and Vyasa had spared some thought to the future management education which seems to be critically dependent on this activity.

How did the young Adi Shankara give feedback to his illustrious guru Govindapaadaa? Adi Shankara completed his education in his early teens and in the remaining part of his 32 years of life he used his education to achieve things which can only be imagined.

However, one theme runs pretty strongly in these puranic stories – filial obedience. For example, the most famous is that of Ekalavya. With some exceptions, like that of Karna, who was cursed by Parasurama for obtaining tutelage by lying under oath. Reminds one of modern courtroom goings-on.

This background is not suitable for modern views on feedback. The current times misuse concepts of egalitarianism. Adi Shankaras views on the 'contextual validity' of research propositions will surely negate the concept of student feedback to teachers. But then, these are days of 'customer is king', despite a lonely voice from the likes of Nayar from HCL who holds employees as kings before the pretender to the throne, the customer.

To carry on with the subject of feedback, it is an outcome of the PDCA view of life, instilled into the operations management curriculum, and hammered into practice by TQM and BE (Business Excellence as exemplified by the Malcolm Baldrige and the EFQM, and many other similar performance excellence models of recent times, i.e., after 1987). The feedback was applied through the mechanisms of customer satisfaction measurement, employee satisfaction measurement and so on. The leadership feedback methods were then introduced, perhaps with the idea of bringing 'leaders' at par with other employees. 360* feedback, peer feedback all became popular. All these developments took place in industry where the relevance and context were competing with others to obtain business. Feedback will lead to continuous improvement, which, in turn, will lead to higher market share, premium prices and hefty profits. These are the positive outcomes which were emphasised, providing the 'context' as referred to by Adi Shankara, to make feedback acceptable to both the feedbackers and the feedback receivers.

Now when we transplant this method to the teaching industry, we need to define the context. Is it that professors are competing with each other, vying to get to teach as many students as possible? Or is to enable deans to keep a hold on the teachers by making it a part of the evaluation mechanism? Or is it to enable the customers, the students (this is a misguided application of a terminology, an outcome of the capitalistic view of all life as 'business as usual") to get the suppliers (the teachers) up to standards?

With a multiplicity of objectives, each constituent giving feedback uses the instrument as suitable to the objectives as defined by the constituent and not necessarily as a way of improving the overall atmosphere prevailing in an academic institution. So, what needs to be done to improve the method of giving feedback?

As usual there will be as many views on this subject as there are practitioners. However the best practices could be:

provide training in giving and receiving feedback; hold open sessions between the feedbackers and feedback receivers, in a transparent way, to exchange views of what went right, did not go OK and what can be done; feedback receivers to discuss the overall situation with the program heads in institutions; compulsory video recording of all teachers of their sessions (or at least some of the sessions, randomly chosen without prior intimation) and specific sessions devoted to discussions by faculty using the summarised issues identified by the Program Heads. I think this process will succeed in what Bill Gates wanted – to create the best teachers.

All power to the feedback process, may it thrive and succeed.

## Curriculum development – a continuous headache

The modern world revolves around education. Many learned people have pointed out that India has remained backward mainly because of our low levels of literacy. This may be one way of keeping the uneducated masses continuously under the thumb of the 'learned people'.

Today's world can be divided into three parts – the Learned World, the Trying World and the Given-Up world.

The Learned World is obviously at the forefront of education. This world has mastered the art and science of educating its populations and, using the benefits of organised learning, clearly established on utilisation of available resources, converting them to useful products and services and driving up standards of living. This world has successfully created a 'high consumption, living for the sake of a high standard of living' syndrome, according to which the more profits a capitalist makes (and shares some of it with the 'Aam Aadmi') the more development is inferred to have taken place. The more one is able to consume, the more is the sales, more is the profit and so on, goes the 'economic cycle' which benefits the common good. This world has developed a 'curriculum' for education and life which are centered on gathering knowledge and using it for economic benefit, for the common benefit. In Aristotlean terms this is the 'knowledge' society, corrupted by the lure for lucre. It is a unidimensional world of money running after more, like a bank willing to lend to someone who can assure that he has enough of it to return the same, after paying interest!

The next world is the Trying World. This one tries hard, trying to catch up with the Learned World. In this effort it gets a lot of guidance from the former, simply because the First World believes that more the merrier and wealth can be shared and poverty can be spared. I recall two views about this dichotomy. The illustrious man manager Russi Modi used to hold that 'managing wealth is more difficult than poverty'. He said this in the context of Tata Steel earning record profits when he took over as its Managing Director. Others have opined that while wealth can be shared, poverty has to be endured. It can be no one's argument that any human being should hold poverty dear and that he should starve because he has no wealth. Printing currency and suffering under the dual burdens of inflation and deficit financing is any day better than missing a meal every other day. However, the Learned World will not allow this. And the Trying World will not dare to defy this. This is a mystery of economics. The most wealth creating country – the USA - has the highest levels of deficit financing – and lowest inflation rate for decades. It also has the distinction of others holding more shares in its industry than its indigenous investors. Japan, China, Saudi Arabia and UK hold more stakes in the USA than the 50 United States.

Coming back to our subject the Trying World tries to go through the same path that its illustrious leader has done without sparing a thought that it is not economic development, but a decent and enriching life is what humans are looking for. It is obviously struggling and does not realise that by the time the 'catch up' act is over there will be nothing to catch up to! The rate at which the Learned World is consuming thoughtlessly, the world as we know it will soon be gone. Thus, the Trying World needs to find other ways and a new idiom and paradigms for world in which life and parameters will be totally different. Days are not far off when the human race will have to migrate to Mars and other planets which are more hospitable to life in the human form. Thus, a new curriculum has to be developed.

By this logic what of the curriculum for the Given-Up World. Does it have to give up on developing any curriculum at all? Not so. In fact, this world is the one which will have to carry the torch (or whatever) after the changes take place. What will be left? Difficult to imagine but management and managers will continue, hopefully delinked from the capitalistic philosophy as the sole arbiter of good and bad, beneficial and harmful, as has happened with the current Learned World. One needs a more balanced view. One needs to use other parameters to measure 'development'. The new world manager will be one who will be trained in fields such as Philosophy, Music, Politics, Public Affairs, Media, Sports which are currently out of the curriculum. Knowledge should be the primary driver. Practice can follow. It is often not appreciated that the only time a management student can legitimately pursue academics is the MBA school, because after exiting, he or she will get into the so called 'real world' with its rough and tumble, leaving little time for academic knowledge gathering type of activities. Only by broad basing the curriculum, deepening the knowledge base and emphasising hard work and work ethic can the managers from the 'Given Up' world manage the world that they will inherit from the clutches of the Learned World, with the Trying World being bypassed, as this world will only try and follow and has no ability to lead. In spite of Ratan Tata constantly and consistently exhorting his group company CEOs to 'lead, not follow'.

So, there are exciting times ahead for curriculum development. Hold on, the flight is about to begin, under new skies.

Chapter 2

# The Changing World of Manufacturing

## The manufacturing industry in India – what ails it?

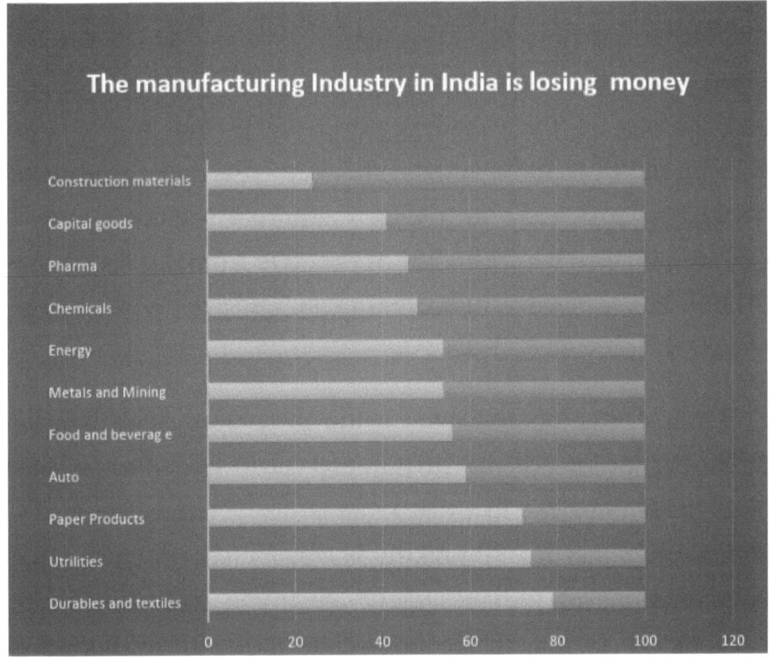


(Source: http://www.mckinsey.com/business-functions/operations/our-insights/fulfilling-the-promise-of-indias-manufacturing-sector#0)

According to a McKinsey data the Indian manufacturing sector is not returning the capital over the long term – and therein lies the rub (see figure above, which shows the percentages of companies in each sector which are returning capital – the first part of the two-part bar). The overall picture, according to the same study, is that more than half of India's manufacturing industry (54%) do not return their capital. The overall average ROIC has been -12 %. You will agree this is not so good. However, there is still hope.

Ever since the British set up their textile mills and other industry in India, an economy which led the world till about the 18th century purely on the basis of agriculture, had to learn about doing business in a different way. While the industrial revolution started in Britain in the 18th century, the US was the place where the action shifted from the 19th century. Europe and the rest of the world got into the picture much later. But, by the time India entered the race 'fish and chips' were stacked against it. From a largely agrarian society, which it still continues to be, with 17 % of the GDP from this sector, the country has to change to becoming an industrial powerhouse. Not easy.

While China has managed to do this, along with Brazill, India and the rest of the BRICS are yet to find their mortar. Notwithstanding the fact that India is the 7th largest economy, and much higher if PPP ranking is considered, the fact is that large sections of Indian society are mired in poverty with no hope of succour in the immediate term. Infrastructure is pathetic, roads are winding their way to nowhere, railway is trying to speed up – and there is no relief in sight. Will it take another type of revolution to make India a superpower? In the Indian context India can be said to be a superpower if it can bring poverty to less than 10 % of its ever-growing population. Tough ask.

No wonder the manufacturing industry has not been able to play its legitimate role in this blame game. Will manufacturing lead the infra or will it be the other way? In the latter case it will have to be a long wait, if at all. It has to be a concurrent effort with the attendant problems and difficulties. To unsettle things, we have the spectacle of the services sector in India growing by leaps and bounds. In the last sixty years the loss of agriculture has been at the expense of services. (see figure below)

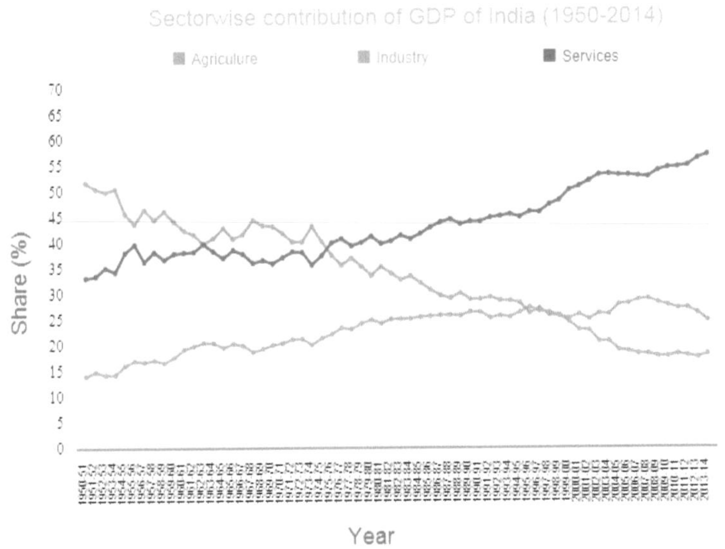


The problems of the manufacturing industry are the classic 'initial stage' variables – poor infra, lack of skill, work neither described nor organised well, the individual vs the collective, lack of use of new technologies and, finally, the lack of a manufacturing culture which is data driven rather than individual driven. For these changes to happen Indian industry must embrace the tried and tested management techniques like

TQM and Lean under the umbrella of business excellence. What is noteworthy is that since the west has taken a huge lead, and the growth in its markets are maturing, as well as the fact that the developing economies present the new growth areas, it has decided to open up its intellectual and industrial knowledge capital to the rest. Thus, knowledge on TQM, Lean and BE – TLB, in short - are all available easily. It is only for the senior managers and captains of the Indian industry to decide to use and apply these.

There is a caveat, however. In India the services industry is booming. But traditionally this industry has been a laggard in the application of TLB all over the world. One hopes that the services industry in India will embrace the TLB culture and positively influence the manufacturing sector – and not the other way around. The Indian IT industry can provide the lead in this. After all the present MD & CEO of TCS came into prominence by developing applications and processes in his company through Six Sigma for GE.

It is here that the latest trends in governance are going to be very helpful. An emphasis on development rather than on the caste and gotra that one belongs to, an action plan to skill India, to build a new India, to Make in India – this is the vocabulary that is needed. Reduction in subsidies, empowerment of the rural population through the direct transfer method, ease of doing business, control and elimination of black money will all lead to a new India which will energise the industry to take up the three methods – TLB - to drive their operations to new levels of competence and high performance. This is so because the golden age of quality was ushered in by only one entity – customer.

Let's hope the relevant people are listening to the call of the times and do the needful.

---

## The changing world of manufacturing 1 – changing by the dozen

IN a highly connected world, the world of manufacturing is on a mission to rediscover its relevance and importance. The winds of change keep blowing, never for once relenting in their speed or intensity, sometimes they may be subtle, for example, when the changeover form 1G to 2G was done, but sometimes violent, for example when the atom bomb was discovered, which changed the potential nature of wars which could be waged in the future.

Prior to the industrial revolution it was the age of the artisans who blew the wind, using a leather windbag, through a pit of burning coal to heat and beat a piece of iron into shape. Along with the potter, the tiller, the milkman, the shepherd and the cowherd they all ran the society along a set of lines where the individual was the prime mover. Dignity of labour, earnings from wages for which one personally worked with one's own hands in shaping the needs of and catering to the societal needs were the norms.

The steam engine blew the whistle on these pastoral scenes and ushered in a new power – that of organised labour. Man discovered the market, discovered that goods could be made and sold in bulk, could be used by a mass of people who may or may not be known to each other. The developments that took place after this seminal event slowly changed the concept of 'dignity of labour'. No more was the workman known for his skills and mastery as an individual – but he became a part of a collective, which, together, as an organisation, defined the new rules of engagement. Manufacturing came to be the centrepiece of the value adding chain of activities which gave rise to products and services.

The first wave of automation swept the manufacturing when Henry Ford designed and successfully ran the assembly line which ran without interruption, round the clock, and workers were told that they could be, at best, cogs in the wheel. Followed by companies like Toyota which used robots to weld, paint, cut and such other operations in an automobile assembly line. The next was when many of the so-called 'low or non-value-add operations' – cleaning, sweeping, moulding, forging, casting, cutting, drilling, planing, grinding, surfacing etc were partially or completely taken over by automatons, pushing the worker to corners where, slowly, only darkness was the visible end of the tunnel scenario. More and more persons were made 'redundant' or 'non-compulsory' and the 'dignity of labour' further eroded. No more was doing a job of a carpenter, a sculptor, a chiseller 'valued' for their individuality but only for their contributions to the final, finished product.

The wireless world has transformed the world into a connected, seamless, single monolith where a person sitting in a design centre in Asia could see the changes needed to be made in a machine in the West and using the standard protocols make these changes and get acceptance through emails and WhatsApp's and Twitters and

Facebook posts. People are more available on the iPhones than on one-to-one conversations and discussions. Indeed, with the Internet of Things on the horizon there is a visible breathlessness in manufacturing. Not only will many of the current jobs vanish but the new ones will need different skills, different languages, different means of communications. The usual banter between workmen and their supervisors and the management team members will vanish too, to be replaced by computer print outs (Virtual), 3D machine outputs, signals through WhatsApp's and robot to robot debates and 'discussions'. More and more workplaces will become like the LD shops and Rolling Mills of steel plants where it is difficult to meet any operator on the shop floor, only one or two mugs looking intently at the consoles, whenever they get the time between looking at their WhatsApp's and Facebooks and internet surfing. Also, like many of our cities where people have stopped going to each other's places but prefer to talk via WhatsApp's and electronics.

In such a scenario manufacturing will have to make changes. What will be affected will be – teamwork, as more and more individuals become empowered through gadgetry to play God; co-ordination which needs a lot of continuous person-to-person meetings and development of a common language with subtleties and nuances which go far beyond mere words; an esprit de corps which needs people to work with each other and experience ups and downs together thereby bringing about synergy and good practices. Replacing all these will be more gadgets, automation run by computer consoles, gadgets connected by wireless connections, putting people further behind machines. With AI, 'neural' networks, big data analytics, man is making it more and more difficult to live with fellow man, eliminating the reasons for interactions progressively.

Manufacturing will soon be less manned, more gadgeted, more connected and driven by AI devices using IOT, analysed and decisioned by big data analytics algorithms and robotised. The only place where manufacturing will still have a connectivity with people is the traditional field of 'customers'. One needs to be cautious here, robots may even replace humans as customers too in times to come. Welcome to the brave new world, indeed.

## The changing world of manufacturing 2 – the advent of eCommerce

There is much in the air these days. eCommerce is riding the waves. So much noise, just like when a new child is born. People want to name it, they want to give special significance to the features, they want to imagine how the child will grow up, how it will change the world and so on. All this has happened in the case of eCommerce, and will continue too. So how to sift the stuff from all the chaff?

Much like the 'film promotions' being done by Bollywood glitterati, eCommerce has been glamourised, demonised, 'God'ditised and revised again in the next cycle. Over the years eCommerce has come to occupy a lot of media attention and space. I am always suspicious of anything about which the media is gung-ho about. You will have to remove the layers to get at the nuggets. You will have to get through the hyperbole to know kya actually bole?

There are at least four effects that eCommerce has had on manufacturing which have profoundly affected manufacturing and changed it forever. To begin with the scale of sale or the volume effect. eCommerce companies are now placing orders which beat the erstwhile 'big' wholesalers hollow. In the 'good old days' a wholesaler had a sphere of influence over an area of say 100 square miles, with a population of about 50,000. If the product which he is involved in is selling at the rate of 100 per person per month, then he would need 50,000*100 = 5 million pieces per month. Adding some safety stocks to this he could be expected to stock about 6 million pieces at any time. Which means that he would order, say, four times a month, asking for 1,25 million pieces per week. In the new eCommerce world, the wholesaler is out of business. The eCommerce company places direct orders on the manufacturer. Since the company's clients base is several millions, merely due to the reach of the website through the internet, the ordering is also in the millions per week. So, now the manufacturer has lesser customers placing orders but the order quantities are much larger. Overall effect is that those manufacturers who have excess capacity are able to produce surges of large quantities and meet with the order requirements and those who cannot are falling by the wayside.

The second is the 'speed effect'. This is a result of the changing nature of buying. Buyers are slowly moving to a space where brand knowledge and experience makes them place orders, the details of which they do not have the time to study thoroughly. For example, I placed an order for a book which has ceased publication some years back from a very famous brand. However, after the promised delivery date came and went without the product, I wrote to the company and they are arranging for the refund. Will I go to the company again? Good question. But more and more such eCommerce sales will happen and customers are expecting goods and services at speed, that is to say, like yesterday. So, if a manufacturer is not able to develop responsive, alert and agile supply chains there is grief at the end.

The third effect is what may be called 'the storage syndrome'. Goods ordered are received speedily, but then the volumes ordered in panic and 'for safety stock' reasons will not get sold so easily. They have to be nurtured and guarded, much like spoilt children, till they find themselves in the hands of a courier or a truck. In this time period they may be tagged, RFID's, GPS'd, vertically handled, horizontally moved, packed, unpacked and repacked and so on. These gymnastics take place in large warehouses where one has to continuously track where the materials you want are. They could also be called Wherehouses. This is a new, major activity, much unlike what any wholesaler in the past has either seen or heard (those who have seen the FedEx or the Walmart DC's will know what I am talking about) and could, over time, become a manufacturing activity by itself. There is good value adding potential here.

The fourth is the 'mind change' effect. Manufacturers are not new to customer returns, but the quantum was well contained, perhaps 1 to 2 %. Practices like lean and six sigma kept defects to the minimum, as a result of which customer returns were less and even, in odd case, high, could be replaced without asking any questions, as the six-sigma process guaranteed less than 3 defects per million. However, the eCommerce customer is a 'mind changer' as many eCommerce retail companies in India have learnt. When the courier reaches the customer after the many twists and turns on the metro roads, using two wheelers which are driven ambidextrously, the customer is unwilling to accept the package as he has had a 'change of mind'. This then becomes the start of the customer return chain which can be longer and tougher than running the marathon as it has to run the gauntlet of the metro roads once again as also the gauntlet of the tax laws which make it near impossible for accounting. So, manufacturers who find innovative ways to deal with customer returns become favourites with the eCommerce companies. But they need to be prepared for returns of up to 10%.

So, if after all these effects, you still receive the goods that you have ordered from an eCommerce company, be sure God is great.

## The changing world of manufacturing 3 – length of value chains

Manufacturing is the ultimate value chain, the chain that creates or generates the values that companies promise to their customers. Value chains are common features where organised activities are done in sequenced, co-ordinated, calibrated, measured ways to create finished products and services.

In Indian agriculture of yore value chains were short due to the fact that all the necessary ingredients were generated at the site – the ploughing field. Manure was made up of human and cow dung, water was from the nearby well, the wooden plough was produced from the nearby trees, and the output was sold in nearby markets through the mechanisms of 'MANDI' OR 'SANTHE'. It was a self-regulating, market driven barter system that governed those early times.

With industrial revolution came the longer value chains. Vendors or suppliers were involved in activities that provided some of the inputs needed for large factories, which could not produce the supplied / vended goods due to a lack of skill or resources or by choice. Oftentimes the perceived risks involved in managing long value chains through long chains of command deterred promoters who cut short the number of links. Thus evolved the broken up, specialised pieces of value chains, which became the model for the production and dispatch of goods and services. Needless to say, such systems, with the value creating pieces at long physical distances from each other, and with large number of persons involved in creating the final value, called for a common currency, thus spelling the death of the barter system. With 'global companies' becoming the norm the day is not far off when the world will switch to one 'Universal Currency' (UC), to wipe out the advantages and disadvantages of economies. Had this happened in 2015, the Donald might have been Trumped out, whose arguments of immigration, off shoring, job stealing etc would have lost their teeth, ground by the UC toothpaste.

Manufacturing was the earliest manifestation of the industrial revolution. The ability of the inventor to come out with various goods which can be used by the market started off a set of activities which were used to convert the invention into a mass-produced item for sale. This process involved machines, tools, man, other resources and management to come together in unique ways and create a totally new entity. Mass production and sales made possible the investment of money into such ventures by capitalists through the profits earned. This 'pancha loka' (or five worlds) was the precursor of the soon rampaging juggernaut called 'manufacturing'. Manufacturing made markets and vice versa. They fed on each other. The value generation or value creation was the pre-requisite to produce goods and services. No goods, no services. Service is merely an extension of the manufacturing activity.

Value chains have, over the years, mutated, lengthened, shortened, widened, covered long distances and deepened through automation, computer usage and connectivity. Mutation occurred through maturity of the pancha loka. Over the years people got adept at building machines. 'Growth' of machines happened in terms of higher volumes and production rates, production of the entire range of components in one machine, sophisticated machines enabled accessorising leading to product differentiation, automation extended the speed range and complexity index, and connectivity has now enabled modularised manufacture and software driven production and controls. More is to come.

Tools have evolved from the basic hammer and tongs to the electronically controlled and operated implements, many of which can fit into small pockets in trousers. They have come a long way. Man has also evolved into a sophisticated creature, which term now includes 'woman' as well (however, the spelling of woman indicates the reverse, such are the peculiarities of the English language), demanding and getting high salaries, perks, work from home options and sophisticated tools to work with.

The 'other resources' list has lengthened and deepened, from power and water to on-tap charging of cell phones, oil and lubrication at the point of application, remote transfer of funds through mobiles. The future is only restricted by human imagination. There is more to come.

Finally, to put together the 'chatur loka' as described above into a meaningful whole God created a voracious creature called 'management'. Ever since the times of Peter Drucker, Peters and Waterman, Edwards Deming, CK Prahalad, Ram Charan, Eiji Toyoda and illustrious others this creature is still evolving and will continue to do so even after the chatur loka will die out. This loka is powered by the human brain and is an ever-growing mutant which will never be satisfied by what it creates, looking for PDCA and continuous improvements, till death and doom do them apart.

Manufacturing is the basis of all value creation and we enjoy the fruits of this all-consuming activity of modern society. Manufacturing links the market with the customer, resources are put to optimal use to maximise output, the right machines are designed and built to add muscle to the nerves of the human brain to optimise the process of creating value. Tools will continue to facilitate the process of manufacture, providing essential background music without which no orchestra can be enjoyed. With digitisation and industry 4.0 knocking progressively on the doors of manufacturing one is in for an interesting epoch of human development. Fasten your seat belts and become a part of the 'march of the pancha loka'. All the best.

# Chapter 3

# It's the Economy, Silly

**Will developing countries ever catch up with developed countries?**

India is a 2 trillion economy now. Britain is a little higher with Germany being a little further ahead. India still remains an anachronism in that more than 25 % of its GDP is from agriculture, while the contribution from agriculture in all developed economies is around 2 %. Our GDP per capita is one of the lowest. In spite of this India is ranked number 2 in terms of PPP! It is as if leading economists took pity on developing countries and found out a metric to give some sense of respectability to some of them, at least. How else could India be placed so high? Scoring high on PPP, in the case of India, indicates that the country maybe poor, but the prices of goods are so low that the population – or large parts of it – is able to make do. Should one accept this evaluation of the economy, because based on this, India has been denied concessional loans from the World Bank and other international development banks?

Even after almost fifty years since the World War II ended many countries are yet to find their feet in changing over to the industrial way of life. While some have made the transition, like some south Asian countries such as Thailand, Malaysia,

Singapore, Hong Kong, many continue to be burdened with high poverty levels, steep population growth, plunging currency parity in world markets and an inflation that shows no signs of flagging. African countries are perhaps the hardest hit, followed by many South American countries. However African countries do not share either a nearness or a border with the US, many South American ones do – and that ADDS TO THEIR PAIN. Ask any Cuban.

In all these countries the GDP growth rates required to catch up with the developed countries are so steep that their leaders have given up on the economy and keep themselves busy with other matters. Economy is a losing game and, as per the old adage, 'success has many fathers, failure is an orphan'. What will happen to these countries? Isn't there any way for these nations to give a better standard of living to its people by rapid industrialisation? Or should they choose some other path – a path which perhaps finds no legitimacy in the current capitalistic orientation dominated western model of living? Should they choose a semi-industrial, semi agricultural growth path?

## The changing world of manufacturing 1 – changing by the dozen

IN a highly connected world, the world of manufacturing is on a mission to rediscover its relevance and importance. The winds of change keep blowing, never for once relenting in their speed or intensity, sometimes they may be subtle, for example, when the changeover form 1G to 2G was done, but sometimes violent, for example when the atom bomb was discovered, which changed the potential nature of wars which could be waged in the future.

Prior to the industrial revolution it was the age of the artisans who blew the wind, using a leather windbag, through a pit of burning coal to heat and beat a piece of iron into shape. Along with the potter, the tiller, the milkman, the shepherd and the cowherd they all ran the society along a set of lines where the individual was the prime mover. Dignity of labour, earnings from wages for which one personally worked with one's own hands in shaping the needs of and catering to the societal needs were the norms.

The steam engine blew the whistle on these pastoral scenes and ushered in a new power – that of organised labour. Man discovered the market, discovered that goods could be made and sold in bulk, could be used by a mass of people who may or may not be known to each other. The developments that took place after this seminal event slowly changed the concept of 'dignity of labour'. No more was the workman known for his skills and mastery as an individual – but he became a part of a collective, which, together, as an organisation, defined the new rules of engagement. Manufacturing came to be the centrepiece of the value adding chain of activities which gave rise to products and services.

The first wave of automation swept the manufacturing when Henry Ford designed and successfully ran the assembly line which ran without interruption, round the clock, and workers were told that they could be, at best, cogs in the wheel. Followed by companies like Toyota which used robots to weld, paint, cut and such other operations in an automobile assembly line. The next was when many of the so-called 'low or non-value operations'– cleaning, sweeping, moulding, forging, casting, cutting, drilling, planing, grinding, surfacing etc were partially or completely taken over by automatons, pushing the worker to corners where, slowly, only darkness was the visible end of the tunnel scenario. More and more persons were made 'redundant' or 'non-compulsory' and the 'dignity of labour' further eroded. No more was doing a job of a carpenter, a sculptor, a chiseller 'valued' for their individuality but only for their contributions to the final, finished product.

The wireless world has transformed the world into a connected, seamless, single monolith where a person sitting in a design centre in Asia could see the changes needed to be made in a machine in the West and using the standard protocols make these changes and get acceptance through emails and WhatsApp's and Twitters and Facebook posts. People are more available on the iPhones than on one-to-one conversations and discussions. Indeed, with the Internet of Things on the horizon there is a visible breathlessness in manufacturing. Not only will many of the current jobs vanish but the new ones will need different skills, different languages, different means of communications. The usual banter between workmen and their supervisors and the management team members will vanish too, to be replaced by computer print outs (Virtual), 3D machine outputs, signals through WhatsApp's and robot to robot debates and 'discussions'. More and more workplaces will become like the LD shops and Rolling Mills of steel plants where it is difficult to meet any operator on the shop floor, only one or two mugs looking intently at the consoles, whenever they get the time between looking at their WhatsApp's and Facebooks and internet surfing. Also, like many of our cities where people have stopped going to each other's places but prefer to talk via WhatsApp's and electronics.

In such a scenario manufacturing will have to make changes. What will be affected will be – teamwork, as more and more individuals become empowered through gadgetry to play God; co-ordination which needs a lot of continuous person-to-person meetings and development of a common language with subtleties and nuances which go far beyond mere words; an esprit de corps which needs people to work with each other and experience ups and downs together thereby bringing about synergy and good practices. Replacing all these will be more gadgets, automation run by computer consoles, gadgets connected by wireless connections, putting people further behind machines. With AI, 'neural' networks, big data analytics, man is making it more and more difficult to live with fellow man, eliminating the reasons for interactions progressively.

Manufacturing will soon be less manned, more gadgeted, more connected and driven by AI devices using IOT, analysed and decisioned by big data analytics algorithms and robotised. The only place where manufacturing will still have a connectivity with people is the traditional field of 'customers'. One needs to be cautious here, robots may even replace humans as customers too in times to come. Welcome to the brave new world, indeed.

## Chapter 4

# The Heart in the Right Place

**Organ donations – what is the way forward?**

Of late organ donation has been in the news in India. So much so that a leading newspaper has started a 'pledge to donate' one's organs. Such movements have been heard of in the past too and they contribute to the overall approach to address a vexing problem.

Organs that fail in a human body and that can be redressed through transplants include the heart, kidney, liver, and, in rare cases, face, hand, pancreas, eyes. Such transplants are the only available solution in the case of a failed kidney.

Kidney failure can happen in cases where the functioning of a kidney is continuously impacted upon by high blood pressure, diabetes, heart conditions and so on. Kidney is a central organ of the body, unlike the hand or leg, whose impairment leads to an overall weakening of all body functions. Since the kidney is a 24*7 clearing house for all the waste matter as also the absorption of vital body building minerals, salts and vitamins, any shorting of its capacity is an undesirable situation, as progressively it will lead to speedy death.

While there are treatments available to deal with a deceased kidney, like dialysis, in the long run, a patient with this ailment will want to get a replacement, to live a full life. Life under dialysis is a slow death.

The problem lies therein. Kidneys for transplant are not available. In view of the reportage in the popular press, which looks at the sensational part of the picture, the laws of the land do not allow any patient to get speedy or even just plain relief in any reasonable length of time. Currently there are only two possibilities in India to get a replacement – either get it from a 'close relative' (which term is defined as siblings, parents) or from a cadaver. Many times, in spite of love and affection, close relatives are not in a position to donate. In cases where such donations are possible the transplant works usually quite well. And the donee is able to lead an almost full life. In the case of a cadaver transplant the chances of the new kidney getting accepted by the donee's body is often a matter of chance. The body can, at any time, reject the newly implanted organ, due to many reasons. In such cases, if the kidney is rejected, the chances of carrying on is nil. Either another is put in or the patient has to die.

The issues in transplant are further complicated by human and emotional factors. The donee is desperate. The donor may not be, and therein lies the rub. The donee then tries to entice the donor with promises, usually monetary. Malpractices, as in anything else, is possible here too. So, what is to be done?

I think the government must come out with a transparent scheme for donor registration and a systematic screening and sorting procedure to allocate a place in a waiting line. Any patient can bid for a kidney. The highest bidder will get the kidney that will suit. The money so raised will go towards a fund which will be used to pay for the registration, maintenance of data, allocations etc. An auction for kidneys will be done based on the availability of 'rich' clientele. The 'poor", or those who cannot afford to bid will be a in a separate queue. The number of kidneys to be auctioned will be decided based on the ratio of the rich and the poor. For example, if the ratio is 10 to 100, then of the total donors registered, one in ten will be auctioned. For every kidney auctioned, nine will be given to the poor / cannot afford category. This is a dynamic system which will be equitable, transparent, and driven by modern technology – online, real time, computerised. Such a system will prevent the current malpractices, make an equitable distribution of the available pool, enhance the pool size in a legal, open way. Donors are free to register without any coercion. They can also withdraw at any time.

It is time that the government took up this work on a war footing. While there are many institutions coming up to provide inexpensive dialysis services, we need to increase the support for kidney transplants as well as reducing the post operations costs too.

# Chapter 5

# Zara sa Hatke or its Different

**IN praise of circuses**

I don't know when it was that you went to the last circus. Not to worry, Even I can't remember when I was under the big dome the last time. Must have been in Jamshedpur many years back, when one was in town for durga puja.

A circus is a great curiosity for a child. The different animals, the large sized elephant, the ferocious tiger, the snarling lion, the tall and elegant giraffe, the beautifully and graciously running horses all create a scene which one is not used to, either in a traffic ridden city or a field filled village. The sight of the many animals, doing several unusual things is a delight for eyes used to track the fumes from a car or ears tuned to the sounds of a smoke belching truck.

A circus is an endeavour only the strong hearted should attempt. For one, the owner has to move along with the tents, animal vehicles, a large entourage of circus artistes of different skills and temperaments, a cash box which has no safety and a car or a truck in which he has to travel which can decide to behave erratically at any time. There is neither scope nor time for preventive maintenance. Truly for every circus owner a training on the various laws of Murphy is a must as he is unaware from which direction what may hit him.

Take the case of Appu Raja. The circus clown is a midget, and he has a band of them, which every circus must have. In fact, the mainstay of a circus is often the comedy routines which really bring in the crowds – mostly children and teenagers – accompanied by adults – and create an ambience of fun and frolic. It is the circus clowns, the comedians and the Joker who enliven the proceedings to keep the show at a spirited level and the audience on the edge of their chairs. The dust, the circus dome / tent which is often of torn canvas and tarpaulin, the various struts zipping criss cross to hold up the large tent, the steel framed cages holding the growling lions and tigers, the odd vehicles on wheels holding the zebras, horses and dogs before they are let out to do their stuff – a circus is a great act of logistics, supply chain management and operations scheduling. Resources planning is critical and efficiency is the mantra for a successful, safe show. Just imagine, the trapeze artistes, swinging from high to low and then again to high miss their swing at the switch!

In all circuses the time when the horses come in is the one which really energises the whole place. Before that the lions, the tigers, whose routines are typically static and full of whiplash sounds, followed by the elephants which try to sit on stools which can't even hold their bums. Then there is an air of speed, the atmosphere gets charged with spirit, then – bang – the cyclists appear with all kinds of two wheelers, three wheelers, four wheelers and set the central plaza on fire! There is speed, there is danger, there is a lot of swishing, with the clowns intervening and showing off their multifarious talents. In fact, the comedians in a circus are the multi skilled individuals on whose shoulders the responsibility of success or failure lies. Like, just when things are trying to slacken off, you hear a loud 'smack', a clown has smacked the reverse of another with a cricket bat or a slim piece of wood, and then the first layer of the pants fall off – and all children are out of their seats, cheering the antics. This is followed by a loud sound, when the motorcyclist revs up for his stunt in the steel globe.

And so it goes. Act is followed by act, groups of artistes followed by another and another, animals and people mix in a myriad of combinations, to mesmerise and entertain, with skills and thrills, truly a variety of offering to animate the mind, to energise the spirit, to tickle the senses, to fill the hearts with goodness and camaraderie. Verily a circus is a great experience indeed.

But lo and behold. There is a 'down syndrome' to all this mirth-making. The PETA! The PETA people are not in sync with all this, they feel that animals are being harassed. Of course, when chickens are being chopped and killed, they are not being harassed, maybe because they are put out of their misery once and for all. So are cattle, lambs and, if you are in China, so are any movable creature. This dichotomy, this irony, this double standard has had an adverse effect on the whole circus business, but I hope that the industry survives and convinces people that humans and animals can co-exist, and do what they can do well. And, sometimes, some animals can entertain some of us, without the PETA or TEPA going up and down.

## Dance shows on TV – to be or not to be?

Recently I saw an article in a newspaper website that Chetan Bhagat has written something about the 'Reality Dance Shows'. The term 'Reality Show' is a contradiction, an oxymoron, with less oxygen than what the 'oxy' could indicate. Participants are pre-decided, they practice their life off, come to the venue fully prepared, some even discuss a few things with the judges, and so on. If this is 'reality' then I will have nothing of it. At best one can say that such shows are 'Live' shows, even that is probably not correct, as they are all pre-recorded. Reality is when things happen spontaneously, when no one announces them, least of all judges them.

I was tempted to read the blog by Chetan Bhagat. I did and was not convinced that it was actually written by him. Don't ask me why, the style was not his, that is my overall view. Still, the point that was being blogged about was that dance should not be judged. If not, then who will watch them? How can someone make money out of them? The whole idea of judging is not to only create some excitement and competition but to create a whole ambience with emotions riding high, with a studio audience (are they coached prior to the show?) seemingly rapturous, aided ably by some of the judges who, as if on cue, do many things to heat up the happenings on the stage. To an extent that sometimes you start wondering whether there is more action amongst the judges than the action on the stage. Changing reality?

A dance reality show is an experience, and should not be judged for anything else. The TRP is one instrument, to which the TV channels pay a lot of attention, but other things, like good dance moves, the quality of the moves, the sublimity quotient, the index of how positive reactions were generated, and, finally, did everyone go home with a sense of wellbeing and goodness, are other aspects which need to be considered. And not get entangled into arguments as to how the judges were poor in their judgment, how the judges did what the TV channel asked them to do, how things were 'pre-fixed' and so on. But you be the judge as to what really happens after the show is over?

While the competition brings about better preparation, newer ideas, revealing newer moves and leads to higher levels of co-ordination, there are other aspects. Chetan blogs mainly based on his personal experiences. But I think that is keeping the circle of experience too close to one's chest and, when blogging about a reality show, some broader vistas could be viewed and used to enrich content. Else there is a fear that the reality of the dance shows may never really come close to reality. Let's keep dancing and blogging.

## Being circumspect

Not to be confused with circumcision. And also, a circle. Then it could have been called circlespect.

To be sure, it is a good quality. To be circumspect is to be careful, avoid pitfalls and embarrassments, ignominy and censure. To be circumspect is to avoid risks, to protect oneself against gaps which can be exploited by the enemy, and in some cases, friends too. To be circumspect is to live life in the slow and often safely travelled lane, keep with the cyclists and give the cars a wide birth, to be as little of consequence as possible, and try and lead a trouble-free life.

No doubt there is much to be said in favour of being circumspect. After he became the PM Dr. Manmohan Singh became so and one could see the consequences. Dr. Narasimha Rao was also one till the day of bankruptcy arrived, and he found the courage to face reality boldly. Foolish bravado and careless conduct are to be avoided as much as timidity and pusillanimity, when you hold positions of power.

Being circumspect makes one shy away from big thoughts, big hopes and ambitions, and setting up BHAGs, in the words of Jim Collins. Big Hairy Audacious Goals are the precursor to achieving big things in life. As they say, if you want to win a race, you need to enter it. You need to knock on the door, only then will the person inside know that there is someone out there seeking entry.

Many of us are afraid 'what will I do once the door opens?'. I recall the years 1984 to 1987 when I was in Bombay House and used to hear eminences like JRD, Nani Palkhiwala, Darbari, Homi Bhabha, SR Subbaraman and others who would repeatedly castigate the then Indian government for protecting the Indian industry for far too long. In fact, JRD often joined issue with the then PM's Nehru and Indira Gandhi on the subject. Was he afraid of what would happen when the doors of the economy opened? Was he afraid that once the doors opened the protected Indian industry will bite the dust against the foreign companies' onslaught?

Having the foresight that India cannot isolate itself from the world (you hear the Donald, the Trump card talk about isolating the USA now) Bombay House was preparing itself to put the hat in the ring. JJ Irani, Suresh Krishna, Venu Srinivasan, Tarun Das, Janak Mehta and a few others were already planning to introduce the necessary wherewithal to combat the forces from abroad as and when the arrivals happen. The arrivals did happen, the wars were fought, some battles were lost, but, in the end courage and vision prevailed over circumspection and timidity. The results show that the foreign powers that be came in with hopes but were tested in the toughest measure.

What really happened? Companies like HM, Mukand, Fiat, Jeep and many others had to shutter or scale down their operations and ambitions, but many survived and thrived. IBM, Coke, Pepsi, P&G, Unilever all came in, some of them did well, others didn't.

Was there really a need for all the halla bol regarding 'protecting' the Indian industry? One can be wise in hind sight, but even 10/20 vision could have sensed that the opening had to happen, and sooner the better. For a civilisation like India, which had survived cultural onslaughts for a thousand years, a commercial insurgency was a mere piffle. You could handle it. To the courageous will spoils of the time go.

Having said that, circumspection is not a bad quality altogether. I get goosebumps whenever I introduce a new course. One is afraid as to what the reaction will be. Will many opt for it? If opted and the course runs, will it do well? There is nothing like preparation and home work. And experience is an added dimension which can be useful.

However, if circumspection stops you from venturing into new areas, then you have stopped growing and learning. Some think that, following the famous Indian cricket commentator Raju Bharathan, 'the team has pulled down its shutters and called it a day', then that's too bad. You must listen to him fully, for he also says, 'we will play for the morrow'. Like Rama said to Ravana in the battle field 'Indru Poi Naalai Vaaraai' (the Tamizh equivalent, in the words of the great poet Kamban, '(you are too tired) go home today and come back tomorrow').

If you have this attitude then you will still survive one more day, if not ...........................you could end up being circumspect forever.

---

## All for a piece of land

When the world began all that was known in terms of organised activity was agriculture. This was mainly because many people took up this way as a way of life. The hunter got tired of the nomadic life, the cave dweller started looking for a sunnier clime, the tribal got bored of climbing trees and picking the fruits for his daily food, and the potter went to pot after several rounds and yearned to switch to a more meaningful way of life. So many turned to agriculture. What is different?

Owning land, for one. Since times immemorial owning land has been an obsession. I have seen many people who ask you – do you stay in a rented house or own it? The moment you let out the secret that you are only a poor lessee the person soon finds other friends, cutting short the conversation. Such is the weight attached to a piece of land. No wonder Leo Tolstoy wrote about the 6 by 6 by 6 land which is only thing that man needs after he is gone, but when he is still alive, he needs 10 or 100 times that.

You have arrived when you own land. Ask any kisan from UP, Bihar, Punjab, Haryana and other states. The story is the same. Do Bigha Jameen, wrote Munshi Premchand. But, over time, in some countries at least, due to heavy population increases the per capita population on a unit piece of land zoomed. More hands wanted to share lesser and lesser acres of land, and tilling became unfulfilling due to the small dimension of the land left over after the sharing ceremony got over.

But the industrial revolution, kicked off by James Watt, brought in a new dimension to using land for purposes other than agri. Soon, over the next two hundred years, beginning about 1780, the industrial usage of land zipped and agri usage dipped. In some countries, like the USA and many parts of Europe, where land is surplus, farmers faced no problems. As long as they confined themselves to the land allotted by the government and did what was good for the economy, they could till their lands and fill their banks.

Due to major advancements in automation and machinery the life of a farmer changed from that of a worker to an owner, ordering and using a multitude of equipment like the harvester, the tractor, the crop cutter and the like. All that he needed to do was to engage some hands to look after his cattle, the fields would be looked after by his machines. He would be looked after by the TV, the refrigerator, the automobile and the ubiquitous pick-up trucks.

Meanwhile in countries like India where land was not in such generous supply, pressure on land came from two directions. The increasing family size demanded break-up of the land to be farmed out to more sons, and, two, industries started demanding their pound at the till. Thus, land got squeezed between these two covetous owners and, as a result, suffered fractures, fissures, cuts and all other maladies that afflict shortage economies. Prices rocketed and availability became an issue. Finders, keepers. But for politicians, others find land which they can then keep.

In such a milieu, politicians, finance ministers, banks all found an outlet for their skills in devising various methods by which a 'suited, booted leader' can tread with caution, but move forward. So now we have a land regime where the farmer appears to be at peace with what he has, mainly because the MNREGA and other such largesse can reach him through bank accounts created through the AADHAR route, long live Nandan Nilekani. While industries are being able to get land through the mega cities route, which are springing up, before we can finish saying Jai Hind.

The pressure on land will continue to fester in India for some more time till someone realises that all resources are finite – land, coal, iron ore, drinking water and the like. So, unless we want to go the way the dinosaurs before us, we must find sustainability, renewability and reversibility. These three terms must now become the new Triple Bottom Line, and economics should take a back seat for some time. If not, in our attempts to keep the economy going by increasing our standards of living, we should descend into an abyss created by those very economic pursuits.

### Where do you work?

Today's newspapers have this news (data released in 2016 of a survey done by the government in 2013): Quote: 'Indians continue to show their entrepreneurial spirit - by opening more and more shops. With over 1.6 crore retail shops in the country, about one for every 15 families, this sector of work outguns every other. Manufacturing, considered the backbone of prosperity for any economy, is second to retail with over 1 crore units. But manufacturing employs over 3 crore people beating retail trade, which has about 2.7 crore.

Transport companies, warehousing, hotels and eateries, and healthcare-related enterprises are other major occupations, while educational enterprises have emerged as major employers with over 2 million such businesses employing nearly 1.1 million people. 'Unquote.

These numbers are not easy to decipher or make sense of. For example, the survey seems to say that every manufacturing unit employs, on an average, 3 persons per unit. If we assume that large corporates with manufacturing facilities are some 1% of the total, with an average of 500 persons, then the data will read: 1 lakhs unit employ 500 lakhs or 5 crores, which is more than the total of 3 crores. Have the media got it all wrong? The Edu sector has over 2 million units with an employment of 1.1 million. Thank God SPJIMR is not included, as, according to this survey, each Edu place employs less than 0.58 persons!

The truth will lie in the fine print, one must read the full report, the media reports are just not good enough. If this is the capability of the media to report on an important survey like this, God save the readers. In the report in the TOI there is a link provided to access the original survey. However, if you click on it, it leads to some obscure page of the TOI archives. Further evidence that sloppy reporting is accompanied by sloppy referencing.

However, the issue that I am worked up about is not whether the media is up to it or not, but whether this country has the jobs needed to employ the youth army that is already at its doorstep. It is heartening to note that the largest sector is the retail, kirana shops.

This is the best example that India is not devoid of enterprise. At every nook and corner there is a kirana shop, pan beedi shop, a small hotel / restaurant, a small general store. These are manned by the owner and some associates who are seen in these establishments. I am not aware of what these shop owners earn or how they manage their affairs, but they are as much important to the country as are the large corporations. In fact, there is a clear division of labour between the two.

The kirana shops play the role of a distributor on a small scale, and many of them pooled together make for the large companies to take an interest to serve their needs collectively as the aggregate demand is sizeable. On the other hand, customers use these outlets because of their small size, their friendly transaction modes (it is easy to get a credit from the kiranas than from any money lender, and you don't have to pay an interest, although the credit is almost always in kind), their friendly neighbourhood appearance and easy approachability. Large department stores are unfriendly, intimidating, depersonalised, although lighter on the purse. Kiranas are flexi, owner driven entities, with strict controls and tight fisted baniyas and other equally illustrious business minded vaishyas who run a tight ship in choppy or calm waters. They are usually grim faced and do not seem to be eager to laugh at your jokes. But then you meet all sorts. The point to be noted is that they keep the wheels of commerce moving. They contribute a lot to the young job seekers and job creators. Only they function in a trishanku – neither the glamour of the startups nor the stuffiness of the large companies. They also serve who run a shop.

# Chapter 6

# Games People Play

## Is BCCI playing cricket?

Shashank Manohar thought that he will play on a different pitch and hence decided to go the nets at ICC. The playing there may be easier, rid of the many bouncers that were getting thrown at the august body BCCI In India, from many quarters. The batting was becoming more and more difficult. To begin with many people were quarrelling with the bat which BCCI was wielding. Many thought that the cricket bat had been changed to a baseball bat, with all kinds of base practices, including stealing bases (this was an old practice in BCCI, nothing new), changing umpires at crucial moments, hitting the ball out of the ground and the dugout becoming a den where players and bettors were interchangeably mixing. Clearly this was not cricket, but perhaps Indian baseball, a new variation of the original.

The baseball diamond was not visible, but Surat diamonds were adorning many fingers of key officials. The great Sharad Pawar, who towered and powered about, for close to many decades had become a pale shadow of his original self. But the other power brokers like N.Srinivasan, Shirke, Shukla, Suman Shekar, Ravi Shastri, Gavaskar, Harsha Bhogle were still around. The CSK scandal was consuming the top batting order, in spite of the many no balls being bowled by Srinivasan. This wily but able administrator, who was the first to bring some sunshine into a cobwebbed organisation, with archaic and opaque practices, began his innings as the Chief of BCCI with many fours and sixers. He brought in the sharing of the booty that BCCI was generating day in and day out with old players, deserving ones, stalwarts who had distinguished themselves in the field and the long-suffering cricket associations which were mere pitching mats and crease powder with the earlier dispensations.

However, his Achilles heel was quite close to home in the form of Gurunath, his son-in-law, who unfortunately functioned outside the law. While betting was rampant in much of cricket with spot fixing, match fixing, ball fixing etc., it was given to Gurunath to bring down his mighty father-in-law. Even big fish like Raj Kundra and Shilpa Shetty escaped the betillotine, but the inexperienced and naïve Guru turned out to be a clueless and meek shishya, with the equally supporterless Srinivasan slowly losing his hold. The final insult was that Srinivasan had to be replaced by a person who was already on his bed, the wily long running horse, Jagmohan Dalmiya. He was woken up to head the world's richest and perhaps most abused cricket organisation, and he had to be helped to walk to reach his office. However, this arrangement lasted but a short time due to the sudden demise of the war horse from Bengal and Shashank Manohar was brought in.

By then the opposition camp had smelt blood and baseball, and went for the middle wicket by petitioning the SC. The opposition camp led by the media and some sports correspondents affiliated to TV channels pushed ahead for the kill and got the Lodha committee appointed through the SC, in spite of no balls called by Manohar and company. The decision of the committee put paid to many of the shenanigans for which BCCI had become famous for by now. For example, to keep out Sharad Pawar a rule was proposed that no person above 70 could be an office bearer. As yet BCCI has not come out with something innovative. This move by the Lodha committee is a straight lift from the Tata book when Russi Modi was ousted.

That was when Manohar played a googly, he eased himself out of the fracas by slithering into the ICC and leaving the BCCI boat in troubled waters. In stepped Anurag Thakur, a brave soul, but a battle-scarred veteran, at a very young age. The SC is, as of now, not playing ball, with BCCI and the two locked in a fierce bouncing wicket which could take a turn for the worse soon. Anurag Thakur and gang could be spun out, could be run out, or could be clean bowled and new batsmen and bowlers called for when the SC comes out to bat for a new innings. Till then we will have a tea break.

### What is cricket?

Why is cricket so popular in India? You may have wondered about this very important question. Important may not be from the academic point of view, but certainly from the multitude of Indians points of view. So many millions of Indians are addicted to this game. I remember once two youngsters were involved in an animated argument, where they freely using every type of curse words under the Sun, frantically waving their arms and legs, emphasising their points using thumps and bangs on the poor wooden table trembling under this onslaught, and I thought that this is a great sign of the times when the young are passionately debating the questions of the day. The youth in India has finally found substance and deciding what is best for the country. Little did I know that the topic under discussion was 'why did Kohli bat at number 4 and not at number 3'? Earth shattering issue, with equally serious impact on the poverty level in the country.

This is just the tip of the iceberg, in a country which has only read about icebergs in the books on the sinking of the Titanic, if that. But you can hear such vociferous arguments in many gullies of India. Gully gully mein shor hain, Cricket India ka dore hain. In fact, I have heard a former Managing Director of Tata Steel waxing eloquent about the strategy adopted by the Indian cricket team to defeat England. I now wonder if this was an item in the Board agenda.

In India cricket is not a game, it is life. A substantial part of many Indians' life is spent on discussions on cricket and also playing the game at many levels. Starting with the compound cricket (where cricket is played within the compound walls of a co-operative society building in Mumbai), to road cricket (where buses and taxies have to stop when the bowler is coming in to deliver his Brahmastra), to cement ground cricket (a euphemism where cricket is played at the junction of several roads where there is a large concrete patch), to the soft ground pitches (from where our world class spin bowlers are born and nurtured), to the maidans and world class cricket grounds like the Wankhede and Chepauk and Green Pauk, cricket is an obsession with dark and white (including those who have changed their colour using the widely advertised dyes), male youth of India. The females are still sitting this one out.

The Indian cricket fan (tornado is a better word, because the amount and intensity of knowledge, arguing capacity, a blind faith in the infallibility of his point of view, all add up to a lot of funnels) has blowing capacity unparalleled in any other part of the world. He can bounce you out, spin you around your hind legs, hit you out of the cricket ground, all in one ball. His knowledge is learnt from the cradle and the womb, and I wish that every nursing home keeps cricket bats along with the caesarean instruments, just in case a male child is born. His arguments can be heard by the mother, like Arjuna's wife Sumitra could. The lullaby perhaps has some cricketing terms of endearment, just to soothe the child by reassuring that India is winning the game, but he can still make it to the team.

The critical appreciation, the insights on the finer points of the game, an ability to keep the listener enthralled and interested in the game and what is to follow are qualities which are displayed by Indian cricket commentators, who, in my opinion, are the best that the world has to offer. To hear a Sunil Gavaskar, a Ravi Shastri, a Sanjay Manjrekar will make you wonder how did these guys get to know so much about this game. I have heard commentaries of NBA, American football, the Stanley cup, ABC. Believe me, these commentators can learn a few things from ours truly.

With the advent of Sunil Gavaskar Indian cricket began producing players about whom one can talk about, quite apart from hearing them comment. We produced some of the best cricketers in the last two decades – Gavaskar, Tendlya, Shastrigalu, Shivaramaiyer, VVS Laxmangaru, Kohli paaji, the Turbanator, the Dhoni of the 'opposition ko dho daala' fame, you name it we have it.

All these facts and figures still does not answer the basic question – from where is the Indian getting his cricket pedigree? One source could be the English blood which flows in the Indians veins. We are so much English, much more than the English themselves, witness the fact that the Right Honourable Srinivasa Sastri was invited to write a new book on English grammar as the British had 'lost it"! Also, there is no place to play other games in our ever so crowded cities. And in the towns where place is available, the people are busy earning their livelihoods using the space for crops and shops. And to let you in on a secret which no cricketer will ever admit to, it is the game which has the least amount of fitness requirements, which essentially means that you can be in the game only as long as you are in the ground. Suits the Indian psyche fine.

Now you know why India is the new cradle for an old game. Rocking truth. Get into it or be left out. The choice is yours.

### Why India is the Champion in Kabaddi

In the recently concluded World Cup for kabaddi in Ahmedabad India once again emerged the champion. Iran came in second. This is one game in which the country has shown its calibre.

Three years in a row. One reason could be because in kabaddi one has to resort to surgical strikes. And these days such strikes have become much talked about and it has come to the notice that Indians are good at it. however, it goes back a long time.

Duryodhana used the surgical technique to occupy the top of the cot position to enable Krishna to sight him first, so that he could get his support for the Kurukshetra war. Arjuna was beaten to the strike, but emerged the eventual winner. But Duryodhana got what he wanted – he was after the Yadava armies and not Krishna himself, who had already declared that he will not take up arms in the war. Should it ever take place, he added carefully. Even in those days quantity was given priority over quality. I wish Boeing had been born many eons before what it eventually did – then its slogan 'Quantity – we can count, Quality – we can count on 'could have been heard by Duryodhana. Maybe the war could have been prevented. But then that would have prevented the declaration of the world's greatest poem – the Bhagavad Gita.

Kabaddi is a game where one needs to be on one's toes, literally. Ones legs carry one to the enemy territory and they should carry one back – only then one can count on points. This is one game where the legs get the highest importance, like in no other game. Not even football where the most famous goal has been credited to the 'hand of God".

Kabaddi is one game where one can – and is called upon to – to pull one's legs. Indians are naturally good at this and this could give them a natural advantage. Pulling legs is an old pastime in India. Yamaraja tried it with Satyavan and Savitri figured it out and pulled her husband out of harm's way. The story of the poor brahmin and the tiger which lured him into the pool with the promise of gold bangles told in the Panchatantra, informs us that as soon as the poor brahmin got into the pool his legs got pulled into the quagmire and tiger got its meal. It is another point of interest, although not central to our blog, that in all old stories in the Panchatantra or any other purana the brahmin is always referred to as the 'poor brahmin', no wonder that brahmins in Kaliyuga are thinking to improve their lot.

Pulling legs is an ancient occupation. When one bathes in a river or a pond one must be very careful. Once I had been to a small agraharam near Tiruchi, where we had gone for a divyanaamam concert with our guruji. We had to go to the cauvery for a bath and I stepped into the river with a prayer in my mind, but misjudged the current velocity and the sudden drop in the height under water, being totally unaware of the floor profile of the riverbed. My legs got pulled swiftly by the current, had I not held on to the towel thrown in my direction by my Guruji, they would have had to pull out only my body. I pulled my legs out in time and escaped certain death. Pulling legs can be serious business.

Is there any relationship between the art of pulling legs and the Indian's ability to survive the vicissitudes of life? Take the case of that quintessential Indian – the Indian politician. Much maligned he may be but he has learnt the art of pulling legs to a fine point. He can pull himself out of any situation, witness the cases of Raghubir Yadav and Rocky Yadav, of recent news mentions. These are only the small fry; Lalu is perhaps the best example of the survivor politician who has pulled not only legs but everything else to keep himself in power and pelf.

Getting back to kabaddi I am sure the western countries are now busy plotting how to pull the rugs from under the legs of the Indian teams. Recall that when we were the best in field hockey, they pulled out the field from under us, put in the artificial turf, to suit their style of play – muscle (many times built up through steroids and drugs) and brawn, and then got thirty years + advantage. Indians were too poor to lay these turfs and practice. It was all done with great finesse. They couldn‘t do it in cricket because of the BCCI and our financial strength. So, one way to keep your legs from being pulled is to be strong and mighty. The world is still in the ‘might is right’ mood.

# Chapter 7

# A Bit of Humour Does One a Lot of Good

## On a Sunday morning, the to-do list and other matters

Sunday mornings are always looked forward to. One, it is after a Saturday. After a busy week. Two, it is the day when you decide to get some catch – up work done, based on the to-do list which is usually drawn up through the week. Shops have to be visited, deep corners of the house have to be cleaned, friends who you have not met in the last few years decide to drop in, and, finally, you need a break from the serious lectures that you have been giving in your classes, and from which you need a big relief.

No doubt every Sunday brings in its wake some new experiences, although you would wish that these would be pleasant. Like the other day I finally sat down to read the paper. Nowadays reading the paper is not anymore, such an important activity, as someone or the other has the TV going. Someone has read somewhere that TV means Together Viewing and wants to experience the truth of this particular expansion of the acronym. So, the TV is always on and the viewers come in go out as per individual need. However, the newspaper reader is caught in all this activity and is prevented from the pleasure of reading the newspaper undisturbed and in peace. That's one time when you can express your feelings freely without any interruption or counter views, of which you have had plenty in the class.

I remember, the last time I had said that students can bring their laptops to the class, the whole class wore a festive look. It was as if someone had released them from confinement. Immediately I noticed that the interest in my lecture, already at a critically low level, was plunging further. So, I said that the idea in allowing the laptop was to enable students to look at the EXCEL file that I had circulated the previous day, so that they can follow the intricacies of inventory carrying costs. The responses ranged from 'the file isn't opening' to 'Swaziland and Mongolia, the only two countries left to address Pakistan, are on the TV airing their views'. I knew that I had opened the Pandora's Box and that the consequences could be unnerving.

As soon as you get through the newspaper there is a rush of items waiting for your attention. This was the day when the tap in the kitchen washbasin decided to leak, and it became a big issue. The water wouldn't stop and I couldn't get the plumber soon enough. After some discussion on the telephone when he finally agreed to grace our house, amidst much grumbling that members of the society should write in the complaints book and not call the plumber directly, he looked at the tap and gave a gasp. Even his trained and tired eyes could not deal with the generous outflow, it was as if the tap had decided to punish the house owner for the years of use and abuse. I made up my mind that day that I would never close the tap too tight in future, maybe that was the reason the tap was so angry with us.

Soon the plumber changed the washer, but not before everyone in the house had had a close shave with a Titanic like situation.

After this drama which had poured much water over the to-do list for Sunday, I went to get the vegetables. This is a chore which you think you can get done in double quick time, but you could be surprised. As soon as I reached the vendor's shop, he asked me why I didn't show up last week, he had kept my favourites – brinjals, spinach and batatas – in a bag, ready for departure, but then had to unpack and sell at a loss. Not only that, he wanted to know all about the incident that had happened in my neighbourhood. I got released after some 45 minutes, but not before he had clearly told me his views on the ongoing struggle in Uri, the hard attitude of the Chinese (he promised that he will never import any veggies from China) and the problems Obama is facing in Charlotte.

And so it went, like any Sunday. You plan to do somethings and someone else has other views. Your to-do list could become to-be-done-next-Sunday list. Long live democracy.

## Indian TV and Politics – Indian ishtyle

Not a day passes without a major event happening in Indian politics. To put first things first. What does one mean by a political event? Will the interview in which Rajdeep Sardesai asked Sania 'when will you settle down, when will become a mother?' and then tendering an abject apology qualify as one? Salman Khan makes a one-line comment which was probably heard by a few persons surrounding him and the whole media circus gets rolling. Now the whole world knows what he said, and is anyone the wiser? All that may have happened was that his film Sultan may have sold a few more tickets.

Then there is the story of the beef controversy in UP. No one knows when will this end, where this story is going, why the court is involved in all this (maybe the judges have nothing better to do, in spite of the mile long queues of cases in all courts). Poor Akhlaq, his family may never have bargained for the TV time that the matter is getting. And what the TV does through the day is faithfully reflected in the print media. So, one can get the idea that a piece of news generated can be profitably used in two media and no one is the wiser - in both media channels the advertisements are flowing in.

The background static, as they say in electrical engineering, is the daily occurrence of a 'terrorist' event. This has become the fastest growing segment of TV media frenzy. Channels fall over each other to 'investigate' (and report within the next few hours, irrespective of how deep the matter is) and 'Break' the news. Incidentally if I see another 'Breaking News' I would be tempted to break my TV.

All of these indicate that the TV and media have lost their marbles. We are all aware that the TV media is far more vocal and penetrative than the print, because Kaliyuga has advanced in age. The first TV pictures were seen by Dhritarashtra courtesy Sanjaya. He could see the war in all its gruesomeness and, if his reaction is any indication, TV is a powerfully impacting idiot box. For such a key transmitting medium to lose itself in the labyrinths of trivia and the sensational means a loss. A huge loss. You never get to know how the new LED bulbs have created a revolution in the countryside. You never hear about the cleanliness drives and how the city of Alappuzha looks like, having been declared the cleanest city in India.

Wake up TV, take your job seriously, and stop this politics Indian ishtyle. Get to meaningful and insightful, entertaining and engaging stuff.

## Driverless Cars, Pilotless Planes, Contentless Books and a Soulless Life

What's going on with the world? The media hype is now on to driverless cars ever since Elon Musk announced his intention to remove the driver from the front seat. Appears that Elon was having difficulties in driving or learning to drive, so he decided to remove the obstacle.

I remember the way I learnt to drive. My father owned an office car much before many others did and I was an avid observer of how a car is driven. We had a driver who was an expert and he could negotiate his way out of many near accidents. These were good lessons, never to be forgotten. So, the way I learnt to drive was to ask one of my sardar friends (his father owned a taxi and he and I worked in the same department in Mukand Iron) to sit beside me in the front seat, and I inserted the key and got the carburettor to kick on. And the rest, as they observe, is history. Elon obviously has a different history.

I am not sure why people are so against their fellow beings the way Elon is after drivers. Google is making a mistake by following the road less travelled, by following Elon. Soon we will have lensless eye glasses, eyeless vision and so on. I am not sure where these people are coming from. Ever since James Watt drove the steam engine industry has been trying to get people out of work. Mindless automation, robotification in the name of removing drudgery, internet of things to get rid of everything else, I suppose.

To begin with, in order to raise the living standards, industries created jobs. As soon as a few people started earning a decent wage and drove themselves out of poverty, the self-same industrialists got into top gear to invent and innovate ways and means to get rid of these earning members of the society, those for whom industry was created in the first place, by automation. Although most companies justify automation in the name of faster growth and defending against 'competition' the truth us that a capitalist does not want to share his wealth. He would rather spend a few millions on inventing more robots, to displace a whole lot of people who earn a few thousand dollars. In such a deadly quest they are assisted by their bean counters who have invented things like IRR, ROI, payback, ROCE etc to make sure that the job losses continue and companies relentlessly stay on the path of making people jobless, the more, the better.

In such a scenario a jobless job, a classroomless education, a friendshipless society are all within the realms of possibility. No doubt Elon Musk, and, more recently, Ford, the company which invented the automobile and whose founder Henry Ford made the first assembly line produced car so that more people can own and drive cars, are hell bent on removing the driver. Doesn‘t matter that the first prototypes met with accidents and were rendered motionless. We will soon see rudderless planes, chipless computers (INTEL nowhere), topless attire (witness the recent demonstration in New York by women who went topless to make a point that they should have the freedom to do so to get equal with men who are allowed to go topless) and spokeless wheels.

Automatic signals, tubeless tyres, hydraulic handsfree operated windows, auto gear systems – have all been seen in cars over the years. People didn‘t notice much these developments which they thought were advancements in technology being put to good use. Whoever imagined that one day we will have the driverless car?

Seriously what would happen if driverless cars did become a reality? Men will be out of another work which they thought was a good occupation. It helps them in gulping down bad coffee during the long morning drive to the office, takes away a genuine excuse that they were ‘held up in traffic’, takes away the ability to feel in command of something after the drubbing received at home from various quarters, reduces the feeling that they can control something which cannot hit back or talk back or, as in this case, drive back, removes an occupation like taxi driving which then reduces the right of taxi drivers to go on strike whenever they feel bored or threatened.

One would hate to imagine what would happen to autorickshaw drivers in Mumbai? They would lose the chance of saying NO to many prospective customers, which will make them feel unwanted and lost in a big, bad, directionless, driverless world.

In short, by trying to remove the driver, the world is going towards an era where 'control' would pass away from humans to machines FINALLY. No going back or getting back. I rest the case. Amen.

## The world of agony aunts, personal counsellors and an unsettled mind

Many of us read, openly or secretly, agony aunt columns where the aunt offers advice to lesser minions who have dared to share their problems openly (semi openly, one might say, as the identity is never fully revealed in a newspaper where such columns usually appear. The names could be fictitious, the problem could be half-printed, the contents of the problem could be altered for dramatic effects and so on). In such a world the job of an agony aunt is never easy. In fact, if you happen to speak to one you might find some peculiar behaviour – she might keep on asking you many funny questions, like, when was the last time you brushed your teeth with talcum powder, when did you last meet your husband etc.

I sometimes read some of these columns and enjoy the exchanges. There are really many women – and men, no doubt – who have issues to deal with which sometimes get a bit too much to handle. So, then they seek the help of an AA (agony aunt) who can a lend a shoulder and an advice.

Take this case, for example. 'Question: I am a 40-year-old woman staying in Mumbai. I have a reasonably happy married life for the past 10 years. My husband provides all the basic requirements of life, the only glitch being the fact that there is no transparency in our lives. I tell him about my day in detail, but he has built a wall around his personal life, which I am not supposed to knock on. When I try, he loses his cool for days together. I cannot touch his mobile phone and all hell breaks loose if I check his WhatsApp. I cannot even ask where he'd been the whole day. Our conversations are restricted to only general communication. No jokes, no laughter and no sharing......... Should I accept this as his permanent nature or opt out as I feel I am allowing myself to be used? - By Anonymous'.

You get the photo, a clear case of defining boundaries, but, more importantly, the havoc that can be caused by something – a cell phone, in this case – which was specifically designed to improve communications through a constant connect! How can this instrument, purportedly invented to connect people lead to a total disconnect, tension and break out all hell? And now by involving an AA the broken connect is sought to be reconnected. In the good old days, you would have had to wait near the neighbour's phone to receive a phone call, but nowadays you can switch on (if it is ever switched off) your cell and reach out. In spite of such advancements in peaceful technology uses tensions can still prevail. Also observe the name of the sender has been protected by 'Anonymous". The question may very well have been framed by the AA.

How would you respond? The answer is simple and clear. However, if you were an AA you wouldn't want to give an obvious answer straightaway. That's not good for business. A straight answer will not give anyone any handle to twist your answer and respond, like the media does. You will have to miss out on all the controversies and the opportunities to stay in the limelight. So, what you do is to raise some further questions so that the conversation does not end immediately, and there is a chance or two of follow-up queries and reverts.

So, you ask: how are you sure that he is shutting you out. Have you checked and found out whether his boss has fired him in the recent past? Whether his driver has asked for a large loan for his daughters' marriage? Or his dentist has denied treatment for a semi broken tooth, till it doesn't fall off on its own? And then insert some suspense: in the next two days please observe his behaviour closely and constantly. Check whether he is receiving calls from this phone or does he have another cell phone. This one is a clear winner: you have brought in the idea of another cell phone where none may exist, but then the suspicions in an already suspicious mind will be heightened.

And then you go on to answer her query: notwithstanding anything that I may have said, which by the way you must do in the next two days and get back to me, I suggest that you should not lay a lot by the cell phone. Please appreciate that the cell phone is the last resort of a man to contain secrets after marriage. Before the advent of the cell phone, he would have to confide in his paramour, now at least that is not the only solution. You should therefore thank the telephone company in your mind and watch and wait for further developments. In the meantime, you should also use your cell phone in a suspicious manner in his presence so that he becomes curious. Then you can have a quid pro quo situation wherein both of you can share your cell phone secrets. After all life is all about give and take.

And you close the whole episode by signing off: hope you will soon find out all the 'secrets' which may be nothing more than the address of his special shirt store, WhatsApp's with his friends on the weather and all matters official. And then go on with your lovely marriage for ever. All the best. Yours truly and always, your agony aunt. Amen.

Long live AA's and their customers.

---

## A Chinese professor and his invention – the lighter side of it

A computer teacher in Chinese B School has found out a method to read the degree of attention a student in his class is paying to his lecture. An Editor of the TOI has thought it fit to print this gem in the edit page of the September 15th Mumbai edition. So must be an interesting and impactful news.

The Chinese are ancient people and have to their credit many firsts, like using paper, building the Great Wall and the world's largest dam. Naturally newspapers keep an eagle's eye out for anything Chinese. And, add to that, a student, who is being sought after by many schools especially if he is interested in doing his MBA. Else who will pay for all the money that B Schools spend on their activities?

The Chinese method invented recently obviously involves a sensor to track the facial expressions of the student from which one can get an idea of what's going on his mind. Of course, the risk seeking professor has not encountered the SPJIMR student who can give a run for the professor's curiosity.

Many of my colleagues will agree with me when I say that the classroom in a B School is an evolved entity. It has now three projectors, several speakers excluding the professor, pinup boards (don't get me wrong, these are for putting up stickers for work in courses like Design Thinking), Wi Fi connections, perhaps to remind those who may have forgotten that there is a world hidden in the internet and it cannot be kept away from the student. There are video players, CCTV's (this is not a very popular device as it could capture the professor's antics also, a double-edged sword, so to say), flip charts, white boards and white board markers covering all the colours of the rainbow, collar mikes along with mounted as well as hand held ones so that you can use whichever one of these is working, and the ubiquitous swivelling chair. This last is a touch as it is expected to prevent anyone from going to sleep as the well-oiled ball and socket joint will move at the slightest sign of the eyes shutting. Into this well-appointed classroom the Chinese professor is adding one more gadget, and that too, to spy upon the most important object in the room – the student.

Don't know about you, but by the time I enter at the dot of the bell some of the occupiers of the swivel chairs are deeply busy on their laptops. They expect you to think that they are doing their last-minute touch up of the calculations that they have been tackling since last night in the 3-page HBS case.

Any other thought is simply dismissed with the contempt it deserves. Some are busy in giving finishing touches to the conversations began in the previous session. They have every intention to listen to you provided you have something useful to tell them.

Most B School students are now 'loanees' before they enter your august portals. They are quite serious about what they learn as this facilitates their ROI calculation, that is, what will be the first salary from the job that they can get when they complete their degree, and how soon can they pay back the loan. Most of the students are keen to learn as much as they can from the classes, especially from the internet. In such a scenario the Chinese professor is going to find it tough going indeed. All that I can say is, good luck to him. Do we need more of such risk seekers? You be the judge.

**Using tough words in tweets**

**Shashi Tharoor**

✓@ShashiTharoor

To all the well-meaning folks who send me parodies of my supposed speaking/writing style: The purpose of speaking or writing is to communicate w/ precision. I choose my words because they are the best ones for the idea i want to convey, not the most obscure or rodomontade ones!

14/12/2017 @ 12:26 AM (!!)

Twitterati - some of them, i.e., those who could understand or make sense of – were flummoxed by the latest tweet by the weather beaten and verbose politician Shashi Tharoor. He who went to England and made the literati there listen to some of the toughest, stringentest messages about the long and often cruel misrule by the colonialists. He was avidly listened to, paid no-heed to and then sent back with a few videos in some TV channels, not to speak of the rainbowesque and myriad replays of his speech, which even the PM of India appreciated. Some of the more adventurous twitterati have accused Shashi T of using 'difficult' English words, and that 'rodomontade' went and used another one in his most recent tweet, (incidentally, for those who don't understand what 'rodomontade' means, don't worry, I also didn't, when I read it. Like all others, I Googled it and got it). Fortunately, this time around, he didn't mix up with another farrago. Some have asked why did he choose rodomontade in preference to hifalutin, grandiose and pretentious, which are equally difficult, but would have served the purpose nevertheless. One tweeter has advised Tharoor to continue with his vocabularisarisation. One must meet this guy, to understand where he is coming from.

Using difficult words is allowed in literature, and, in fact, it is the correct place to use them. This enables the reader to learn about the language. Difficult words are used in very specific context, to refine the reference and exclude any other general implications. To zero in on the very specific meaning to the exclusion of all other. For example, if I were to say, this is a quagmire, I want to say it is a quagmire, so as not to be confused with a fen, or a slough, or a morass. Equally, not to be confused with predicament, quandary, mare's nest (figure this one out) and imbroglio. My first acquaintance with difficult words was in the English lessons that one studied in school. I met dromedary, I learnt about a cocoon, the onomatopoeia, the oxymoron, alliteration. In modern times these may not even qualify as difficult words, definitely not by Shashi Tharoor standards, or so I gather. However, in dromedary, I have a winner.

Why does one use difficult words in sentences? The source of this habit could be many. For example, think of an author writing a modern-day scientific fiction, he needs to build in atmosphere, then he has no choice but to choose from terraforming, hive mind, ansible, cryonics, and such. This is what one may call 'use by compulsion". Another reason could be that the author is trying to test the learnedness of his readers. So, he uses, millennials (instead of simply saying young people), cohorts (instead of simply saying a group or division. This word originates from the Roman army. Thus, its basic usage should be when discussing army related happenings, but academics use them in many other contexts, to connote groups, mostly peaceful ones at that!). Then there are authors who use difficult words because their minds are complicated. You may have met such specimens, who have the knack of seeing the difficult in the easy, like India snatching defeat from the jaws of victory. To them, such words come naturally, most of us could stay away and use our time in a better way.

There is this story of how the great sage Vyasa convinced the good lord Ganesa to become the scribe of the Mahabharata. The story goes that when the sage Vyasa wanted to write the story, he had a to find a suitable scribe, as he did not have the modern laptops or typewriters. So, he scouted around and Ganesa happened to meet him. Immediately Vyasa told Ganesa that he should be the scribe as there is no one else better qualified. Sounds familiar? However, there was a catch. Ganesa was a speedy writer, and Vyasa would be hard pressed to continuously provide the sound bites for Ganesa to transcribe without a break. (Something similar to Shankar Mahadevan refusing to sing songs where one has to take breaths between words). This could lead to an embarrassing situation of a mere mortal making the good lord wait. No can be. To the challenge of Ganesa, that Vyasa should dictate in such a way that Ganesa will never have to stop writing, Vyasa set the counter challenge-that Ganesa should transcribe only after he comprehends fully the meaning of the dictated passages. This is the place where Vyasa and Shashi T are in sync. Whenever Vyasa felt at a loss for words, he would dictate a very tough para, consisting of very difficult words, so that, by the time Ganesa understands all that and is ready for the next dose, Vyasa is also ready. So, here we see an example where an author uses difficult words, so that he is able to keep pace with the scribe. A rare thing indeed.

Then there is the famous and mysterious ‘covfefe”, attributed to the great twitterater Donald Trump. No one has been able to figure this one out. The grapevine is that the word is to be included in the encyclopaedia as soon as its purport is ascertained.

You, reader, figure this one out, by which time I will be ready with the next blog.

# Chapter 8

# Generally Speaking

## Surgical strikes – the multipurpose tool for all seasons and all reasons

This surgical strike business has got a life of its own now. By itself, it was a revelation. That an army could, in such a short time, organise a wide-ranging strike to neutralise and eliminate enemy personnel is a striking competency hitherto unknown. And that too the Indian army, which often is held back by a political class which prizes peace over war mongering, and rightly so. India has never stood for war and it will not rely on war as an instrument of strategy. Only after the patience of the people of the country is sorely tested leading to a national consensus that 'enough is enough' and a large part of the international community in concurrence of the general opinion that the enemy has crossed all limits of forbearance should such a strike be called upon. Well done India and PM Modi.

It is a great diplomatic triumph that the international community has fully endorsed and supported the Indian point of view. This is the clear, unambiguous outcome of the various visits undertaken by the PM to far off lands. All those efforts were not without strategic intent. Nor was the master stroke of the quick landing and friendly take off from Nawaz Sharif's backyard during the PM's return from the USA. He also was gauging the power of the generals too. This sudden, unplanned meeting showed that the PM wanted a rapprochement, not war. He was extending the golden handshake, confirming that the invitation for the oath taking ceremony in New Delhi was not grandstanding, it was the first sign that India was open for business.

However the enemy generals misread the moves and thought that they were dealing with the old congress and authors coterie (this seminar and conferences loving coterie included Mani Shankar Iyer, Arundhati Roy, Dileep Padgaonkar, some of the leading lights from Punjab and some freeloading journos who are always on the hunt for freebies and scoops) which, while dealing with great patience, did not show any strategic spine in dealing with and putting a stop to these cross border picnics which seemed to have gone on for too long a time. It appeared that Indian lives did not count for much.

The surgical strikes have been compared to the Israeli efforts. Now this is a different ballgame. The Israelis are at the other end of the spectrum. Due to their situation where they are surrounded by a hostile lot of enemy collaborators, they have to deal with speed, precision and strength. While the Indian civilizational advantage gives it the wisdom to try out peaceful means before finally doing what is needed done, Israel, no less civilisationally advantaged, lacks the numbers or the moral power to curb violence. The image of the money hungry Jew, displayed in the Shakespearean play 'Merchant of Venice', to the flexing of muscles by the powerful Jewish lobby in the US and elsewhere, makes sure that the finger on the trigger is often too unresty. Thus, out of sheer necessity the Israeli military has had to innovate the surgical strike methodology and practice it to a fine art. But then the Indian army is not used to this, and rightly so. However, what needs to be done, should be done.

"Striking activity 'has not been unknown to corporate executives. In fact, mergers and acquisitions have been in vogue ever since the dawn of business. Some of the voracious acquirers include GE, Walgreens, Kroger, Rubbermaid, GM, Ford, Benz, VW. Some of the biggest deals by Indian corporates include Tata Tea, Suzlon, Tata Motors, Tata Steel (Corus, the mother of all deals), Hindalco, Vodafone. According to a report by Mr. Rajat Kataria, (2010) (https://www.scribd.com/doc/53091392/Mergers-and-Acquisitions-in-India-2006-2010) the summary of such 'striking' activities between 2006 and 2010:

| Year | Number of M & A | Total (Bn INR) | Total (Bn USD) | Average value per deal (Bn INR) | Average value per deal (Mn USD) |
|---|---|---|---|---|---|
| 2006 | 697 | 865 | 19 | 1.24 | 28 |
| 2007 | 867 (Including 262 private equity deals) | 1576 | 38 | | |
| 2008 | 455 | 1027 | 23 | 2.3 | 52 |
| 2009 | 355 | NA | 12.5 | 1.027 | 22.3 |
| 2010 | NA | NA | 68.3 | 120 | 100 |

Not bad for a developing economy.

Striking in Indian politics has also been known for long, the earliest manifestations being 'Aaya Ram, Gaya Ram' defections. On many occasions several MLA's / MP's have been 'kept in safe custody' to prevent predators from poaching them. Recently Mulayam Singh used this weapon in a very broad, silken way, so that the guy whose throat is getting cut is still unaware of the threat. Akhilesh apparently has to be reined in. Although another news item talks about the second wife being the guilty party. Lalu is another expert at this. He used this technique effectively to get Nitish on his side of the boat and they row it into the choppy waters of prohibition.

And, so it goes. Surgical strike has now become the buzz word. I hope we don't see more of it but you never know.

## Surgical strikes and the polity

Of late surgeons and surgery seem to have eaten up a lot of mind space of Indian politicians. Some have had to brush up their knowledge of surgery to fathom the extent of the damage that India has inflicted on our friendly neighbour. Surgical strike is an armed forces technical term with a definition and all the attendant descriptions of what actually constitutes one. Most of us civvies perhaps have no idea of what it actually is.

For example, the CIA has been deeply involved in covert operations, spying games, skulduggery and other shenanigans, all of which are well defined in the CIA manual which is kept updated to suit the times. When the master terrorist Osama Bin Laden was assassinated, they had to declare under what category it belonged to, and they said that it was a surgical operation, to perhaps distinguish it from a surgical strike. Nevertheless, the idea was to deny information and dare the world to disprove what the CIA said had happened. (in the case of the Laden mystery, some say that it was an operation conducted by Navy Seals, but then even the identity of those who carried out the operations remains shrouded in cloak and dagger).

In the case of the Indian operations there is a certain background to the whole series of events. The PM went out of his way to make friendly overtures towards his Pakistani counterpart. But he didn‘t reckon for the army general with the same last name. While one may be a real sharif, the other is far from it. In one of the many TV shows the former ambassador to Pakistan Parthasarathi called the other sharif (or is he a badmash?) an egomaniac. PM Sharif came over to India and powwowed with the PM, confident that his last namesake can be handled. However, the Panama incident put paid to all such hopes. That incident was a terrible setback for the real Sharif, as he had to rush to London to escape arrest and court cases in Pakistan which could have easily followed had he remained in Pakistan. He did what his predecessor Musharraf did – packed up and ran away. Although the sojourn was not as permanent as in the case of Mushy. Mushy is now safely ensconced in Chicago enjoying two things – his quota of the spirits and India bashing, both his favourite pastimes.

The real Sharif returned to the country after hiding appropriately all his misdeeds and ill-gotten wealth but with a lower profile, a clear mandate to be subservient to the army, and dance to their tunes. It was under this scenario that the terrorist circus once again started its show, with a well-planned, multi flank attack. Pakistani lackeys in India like Gilani were asked to create unrest through the supply of well cut, sharp stones (reminds one of medieval times, Solomon and Sheba) while the terrorists were trained one last time infiltrate and perform their usual cowardly acts. That the Pakistan army has no dearth of supply of such poor saps is a reflection of the poverty and desperate levels of survival of the lower strata of the society in that land. So, the incident at Uri happened. I don't know whether that was the last straw on the camel's back, but PM Modi had had enough of the Pak army. So, he used the occasion to make a few points.

At this point it may be useful to understand that the actions by PM Modi are well thought out, planned and strategic. All those who questioned his foreign visits now understand the reason. Never in the past have so many nations expressed so much of solidarity with India. The usually glib bunch of Surjewala, Sanjay Jha, Manish Tiwari, Salman Khurshid were at their usual verbosities. I thank all the TV channels that they have finally kept out Mani Shankar Iyer whose barb about PM Modi will surely haunt him for the rest of his life, and Manu Sanghvi. The worthy Salman (of the Khurshid variety) went to the extent of saying that 'surgical strikes are all ok, we (UPA) have also done these, but when are we going to start talking?'. Duh. He seems to be in a tearing hurry to stop hurting his friends across the border.

PM Modi's visits, his genuineness to convince his hosts, in a very short time, of his intent to deal from a position of strength seems to have connected with the westerners. They understand only one language – that of strength. Rightly so. This world is not for cowards. Like the Paki army. The Terrorists.

And this is only the beginning.

---

## Medical insurance and the welfare state

This is a topic that is currently bugging the middle classes in India. Unlike life insurance which has long term implications and hence not considered a suitable topic for discussion in everyday parlance the medical insurance has the potential for discussions and occupying time which otherwise may be passed in slumber.

The concept of medical insurance is a part of the welfare state concept. Like so many modern concepts it is also a product of the western way of life, suiting their unique needs and mental satisfaction of the capitalists who rule the roost, as a salve to their collective conscience. It is the natural outcome of the dominance of the industrial way of life in western societies. Having blocked the government from interfering in industrial activities, the industry owners had to find some way of keeping governments occupied, so that future interferences are avoided.

The leader of the western society, the USA government, chose two fields of activities to maintain its relevance – creating a welfare state and politicking in the international arena where their acceptability is easy to obtain, given the wealth and dominance created by the industrialists. This way there is a legitimate role, acceptable to both the indigenous and outside world. The outside world really has no say in the matter, have you ever heard of a lessee permanently outing the landlord?

One field which western governments fully and continuously arrogate to their active role playing is medicine. The wellbeing of a subject is a matter close to the hearts and minds of the ruled and nary will raise a negative peep. People are often happy that Big Brother is caring for them and will foot the bill. Duh.

Footing the bill is where the nexus between the industry and government strengthens. The bill is prepared by the industry (pharma and chemical industry largely, in this case) and is paid by the government, without questions. With no oversight of the insurance process – simply because, NONE of the stakeholders has any interest in doing so, on the contrary, each of the stakeholder wants to maximise his benefits – it is a situation designed for complete disaster in the long run. Cultural and monetary. Milking the milch cow scenario. But, even Kamadhenu can get tired in Kaliyuga.

When the going is good, why complain? But when the going gets tough, the government and industry get going leaving the hapless insured in limbo. The government, because it has no funds to continue the largesse and the industry because it has no interest in any activity that does not earn a daily profit.

Medical insurance is a total misconception. A better concept, which has been found acceptable and working successfully in the Indian medical field, is 'borrowing from Peter to pay Pan'. In other words, institutions like the Aravind Hospitals have found an essentially socially acceptable, sustainable, equitable model which enables them to charge those who can afford to pay a little more, and use the excess funds to subsidise the cost for those who cannot afford. The good thing about this methodology is that it leaves huge scope for changes that happen in society. As the middle class keeps increasing the overcharging per customer can come down, while, simultaneously, those needing subsidies will also go down as the general economic conditions improve. What can be a better, market regulated, free market phenomenon? But then, we will always like to be led by western practices without a thought to the applicability, the ease of designing and implementing an alternative – and, in this case, a better solution – in preference to blindly following.

Where does this leave the common citizen and the Indian government? The common citizen is often compelled to become a part of the insurance policy funded medical expenses framework while the government is compelled to find alternative ways to introduce insurance policies for the poor, like the Rs. 11 premium per month. Such efforts will continue, for, after all, who can forget the comment by Rahul Gandhi: this is a government of suits and boots (suit – boot ki Sarkar). I find that the Modi Sarkar has completely changed its vocabulary to sing praises of the poor man and farmer and denigrating the rich and wealthy. This is unfortunate and not helping anyone.

I think in the long run it may be better to let the market do the arbitraging, if at all. With increasing wealth, and a good supply of doctors, the cost of medicines should not increase sharply in India, as there is still a large percentage of the population which has not entered the medicine purchasing market. The government should intervene from time to time to set limits on the prices, which overall is a simpler, less bureaucratic and least expensive process for all concerned. It enables the country to get some medicines at low costs (hopefully these are the ones which are commonly demanded) and the others at higher costs, which is a burden which one needs to bear once or twice in a lifetime.

---

## On Leadership

WhatsApp is an active platform, perhaps the most active one, amongst the modern-day public platforms – facebook, emails, blogs, linked in, linked out and whatnot. You keep getting messages which you may not have asked for. Many people take pleasure in forwarding. In fact, WhatsApp has a given a whole new meaning to 'forward', which was once a much-reviled function, witness the many 'forwarded' emails which would be deleted without any fanfare. WhatsApp has changed all that, it has shown how a 'forward' can make sense and be a source of pleasure and information. But that's not what I want to blog about just now, that will be another blog.

One such message I got today from an old friend of mine. He wrote: Lord Rama was a leader, so was Krishna. Rama led an army of monkeys from the front. He himself was a great, mighty warrior, and he directed his forces to do what he had in mind. The monkeys, being not very intelligent or skilful, were happy to be led and followed him to victory. But Krishna was quite unlike Rama. He refused to get into the war, was not known for his prowess as a warrior although his Narayani Sena was a mighty and much feared force. He declared that he will only advice and guide whoever wants to be. Duryodhana decided Krishna's army was far more valuable than the person. This could be a case of quantity over quality. Like the Boeing company's famous slogan: quantity – we can count, but quality – we can count on.

In the war Krishna provided inputs, guidance and also revealed his famous Bhagavad Gita, an exposition on the importance of a way of life. In this case the Pandavas and Kauravas were neither monkeys nor ordinary human beings, but evolved souls who were skilled (at the world class level) and learned, competent and mighty, and it fell to Krishna to provide only strategic inputs and action plans. These are perhaps two extremes of the myriad types of leadership styles that are available to leaders to follow. How does one choose? The short answer is: depends.

Do leaders really choose a style or is it inborn and innate to the person. Did Krishna train to be a strategic advisor? Did Ram Charan or Vijay Govindarajan or CK Prahlad train to be strategic advisors from their birth? Did they know that they will be thought leaders in this key sphere of organisational activity? Not really. It evolved over time, but there has to be a mutual fit – between the style and the individual's talent, attitude to life, aptitude and circumstances.

Take the case of Mahatma Gandhi. Was he a born leader? No. The fateful train journey in South Africa turned a till then docile lawyer into a firebrand rebel. This side of his character is totally missing in his great work in India. He had embraced 'ahimsa' in India. This was a big change. He also was a leader who did not ask to lead from the front. He was pushed into the leadership role, into which he settled down well, and, over the years, excelled. He became the platinum standard of leadership.

In totality he can be called the best leader the world has ever seen. He did not have the might of Rama but he made the mighty British bow before him. Unlike Rama he did not lead from the front, but people liked to be led by him, they asked and wanted to be led by him. Leadership was thrust upon him. To his credit he lived up to the expectations. A lesser mortal would have folded up. Which means that he had the talent, the attitude and the aptitude, the circumstance was of course waiting for him. Like Krishna he was not a 'strategist', with a deep knowledge of life and its mysteries. He was a lawyer by profession, a self-taught man about Indian philosophy, the shastras, the puranas, the vedas, the upanishads. However, his homilies were down to earth and understood by a population which wanted to hear him say those things. One could thus conclude that Gandhi was in between Rama and Krishna.

In conclusion, leadership is a many splendored thing. It can grab you when you are young or when you are not so. Gandhiji became a leader only in his later years, well beyond middle age. Narendra Modi has become a national leader at a ripe age of 60+. Narasimha Rao was close to 70 when he led the country into the modern league of nations. It can grab you whether you are rich or poor. Gandhiji was a rich barrister. But leaders like Narendra Modi, Vallabh Patel, Tilak and Lal Bahadur Shastri were all born in poor circumstances. And we can go on thus.

WhatsApp is sure a great source of thoughtful apps.

## Stock Market or Shock Market?

Very few of us are not tempted to enter the share market. The majority (or the losing majority) is forever itching to try its hand at the hustings. In some unfortunate cases this 'hand' soon becomes leg, followed by the shirt, the pant, the house and thus it goes the litany of woes. In spite of the very few big bulls like Harshad Mehta, Jhunjhunwala, Sucheta and other Dalals, Ketan Parekh who actually seem to make money and then come to grief, many try their luck. It is much like buying a lottery ticket – once bought, return to buy.

What lures people to the stock market, aka shock market? To be sure the lure of lucre. Moolah is what some people are after and the sooner they can accumulate the better. What they don't realise is that, as any operator at the Reno, Las Vegas and Goa casinos knows fully well, you can never win against the house, the odds are always stacked against the individual. Once I played the Over 7 / Under 7, I won the first two rounds, accumulated a decent three figure amount, and then continued. Sure enough the green changed hands and I was left with an empty hand. One should know when to stop. My suspicion was that the croupier allowed me to win and then turned the tables. This is where the dilemma is. The one who knows when to stop also decides never to start!

After the demat system kicked off in India the operators became far more circumspect in trying their antics. With SEBI also coming down hard, it is now very difficult to do the many things that used to happen routinely in stock markets. The demat system has made many punters turn to the share market to 'have a go at it'. Only, they realise too late, they will be the ones to go.

For those who wish to stay the long run the stock market is a hospitable place. While no one has found out the secrets of why the markets operate the way they do, there are some smart people, like Warren Buffet, who seem to have learnt the ropes, and kept it out of their necks. Buffet has consistently beaten the market, but I don't think he has shared his secret, if he has figured it out. There are some important points about the way the markets move. For one, when there is a serious political or economic event the market moves down, and this movement is shares agnostic. When there is a boom even a donkey starts running fast. Dud shares start doing well and sections of punters start getting into these. This is a potentially wrong move. Some punters stick to the BSE 30 or the NSE 50. This is a sure shot policy for long time gains, but such punters, also known as investors, are rare. Take, for example, scrips like Maruti, HUL, MRF, Eicher, Hero, Grasim, Ultratech – some of the stars in the market for many years, although some of the Birla companies are Johnny come latelys.

So, what is the secret of negotiating the stockmarkets without getting shocked? Some tips. Buy into 'good' investment grade shares. In a booming market, sell and shift to new scrips which are on the upswing. In such markets one will have to sense the short-term peaks and sell out at these, and then come back to buy these scrips once again. In short, in a booming market, maximise your profit by scrips hopping and profit skimming. Profit skimming is a method to pull out some part of your profits which you constantly make by scrip hunting, and salt it away on a fixed type of investment like a mutual fund or FD or debenture. This way when the downturn arrives – what goes up must come down – you can lose out on the existing exposure but your salted away kitty will be untroubled. This could be your saviour in times of recession.

The investor will neither buy nor sell at any point – he will buy IPO's from the company through applications etc, and as soon as the shares are allotted, put it into demat and forget about it. Much like what Hero Honda used to advertise – fill it, shut it, forget it. He will live off the market returns – capital appreciation through stock splits, bonus shares, rights issues etc and regular returns through the dividend route. The usual long-term yield for such investors is about 5 to 6 % in the long term and a bit more in the longer term.

The Good to Great companies returned 17 % compounded on their share prices over 35 years, between 1965 and 2000. If you had owned shares in any of these 11 companies, and CASHED OUT at the end of 2000, then you would have received 471 USD per dollar you invested in 1965. Dream Big, but invest wisely, all the best.

## An atmosphere of intolerance in India?

Today's news headlines informed us that Mr. Ratan Tata had, in a speech in Gwalior, in the presence of Jyotiraditya Scindia, expressed concern over the alleged growing intolerance in the country, dubbing it 'a curse we are seeing of late". What prompted him to say these words? Since it is coming from an impeccable source of uncompromising integrity one cannot ignore or brush it under the carpet. One must respect and ponder over why he is feeling that way. Ignoring the warning can be only at one's own peril.

India has been under attack from Pakistan for many years now. All these years the Indian response has been to put up a brave face to control damage and slowly but surely put out the memory of the events, manage the outfall and move on. Making some noises at the UN followed by many seminars, conferences, back-channel talks and other such efforts to once again establish a semblance of friendship. There was nothing wrong with this approach. It was by and large dictated by our thousand years of slavery under various foreign rulers. It is to the credit of the Indian that he never sees anyone as an outsider, but only another fellow human being on his journey through this earth, to attain nirvana or moksha.

He has never ever had any biases or prejudices, on the contrary the culture of the Indian soil has always been athithi devo bhava. This was not a mere slogan, there are innumerable stories in Indian folklore where people have gone out of their way to serve guests to their own disadvantage, given them priority over self needs, always 'shared' what was available. Such was the overall situation that when the pandavas came back to Hastinapur and informed their mother that they have come back from their travels and that they have brought home a treasure, the unsuspecting mother told them 'share whatever you have brought', which is when Draupadi had to become a wife to all the pandavas.

Another issue is the Hindutva brand of politics that has come into practice with the BJP coming into power. For many centuries now, due to the many attacks and persecution, conversions by all and sundry, the country lost its self-respect. This has been in evidence for many years now. At the simplest level of manifestation, many Indians, once they hit foreign shores, change or shorten their names to sound like they have descended from the Anglo Saxons. Krishna becomes Kris, Rama becomes Ram (pronounced as in Ham), Ramaswamy becomes Ramsay. Tell me one foreigner who changes his name. Except the odd one who either through association with Hare Krishna or similar such movements get themselves rechristened.

Similarly, we get very sensitive if Bombay is renamed as Mumbai, in reverence to Mumbadevi. We immediately start pointing out the long-term damage that can be done to the secular fabric of the country. Valid, however the damage that has already been done to the fabric of the nation is forgotten or trivialised. How does a country regain its lost self-respect?

I wish to remind all that India is a civilisation which has been around for many moons and will be around for many more, however it has to be rejuvenated from time to time. Like what Krishna says in the Bhagavat Gita – I will appear from time to time to establish Dharma when I perceive threats.

The last avatar of the God was in the form of Adi Shankara who, in 700 AD, walked the length and breadth of this ancient land of ours, and once again established the truth of the immutable truth, advaita, the oneness and non-duality, only through debates. He was a giant of his times, he has composed such gems of philosophical treatises, that are unmatched even to this day, walked the entire length and breadth of India and established great institutions.

Did he kill anyone? Did he convert anyone? Did he blaspheme anyone? The only person he defeated in his very short lifetime of 30 years was Mandana Mishra, the highest-ranking Buddha Bhikshu of his times, who, after the defeat in the debate, became Adi Shankara's first disciple as per the terms and conditions of the debate. This is the tradition that India comes from. But how many Indians have heard of him? In how many schools and colleges do we read about him? On the contrary a whole host of efforts is made to ensure that he is never even mentioned in any meaningful manner.

The great Indian culture will fight to preserve itself, but never impose itself on anyone. Fight it will, just like what Krishna said, and great souls will happen in India from time to time to do this. The process of going from the present when the country has disowned its civilizational heritage under the garb of secularism, to the real hindu rashtra, where the only business that anyone has is to find his path to moksha through karma yoga, irrespective of what his creed, religion, etc is what the journey is going to be. Along the way there could be perceptions – backed up by facts – that the pace is too fast or just plain wrong or getting derailed.

We must listen to such wise counsel, like that of Mr. Tata, and make the necessary course corrections and assure them that the movement towards a more egalitarian society, for which our ancient land has been well known, will stay its course.

---

## Why demonetisation? What will it achieve?

The flavour of the month is demonetisation. Learned economists, government ministers, journalists, in fact learned everybody who is somebody is weighing in on the phenomenon of the month. Every Tom, Dick and Ram has given his views and his expectations on what this demonic demonetisation move will achieve – and not.

Let's look at the dimensions of this move. In fact, to call it a move is itself a disservice. That a gamechanger of this magnitude has been kept a secret even from all the learned bureaucrats, except perhaps Shakti Kanta Das, is in and of itself a Guinness World record of which we Indians can be proud of.

The predecessor event, which some say emboldened and laid out the way for the Guinness Attempt happened in the largest and most venerated Indian corporate house, the House of Tata. The way the coup was delivered established a Guinness Record in the world of corporate governance. I don't think Cyrus still knows under what Mistry circumstances the blow was delivered by two much decorated men – RN Tata and Nitin Nohria, that eminence from the world's leading business school – Harvard. Now we know why the HBS is world class – it not only theorises, but also walks the talks and knows how to say Tata.

Getting back to the DeMo, it is not important what finally gets done. It is important that such a bold move was actually attempted and done successfully. Now, don't get me wrong and start squabbling – how can I declare victory when there is still a month and a half of time available before the formal closure is applied to this grand curtain raiser. For sure this is only the trailer, much more will follow. I think it will be truly said of the current PM – there never was a dull moment.

He began with a bang, he invited the enemy home, to felicitate and embrace, only to be rebuffed later. He followed this up with the opening of 1.5 crore bank accounts, I repeat, 1.5 crore bank accounts, on the opening day of the PMs.' Jan Dhan Yojana! The Guinness Records Book noted that the 22.5 crore accounts opened in less than 6 months was a huge world record. A new Guinness Book had to be opened, to accommodate more of such stuff!

He then used the surgical strikes to silence Pakistan and isolate it from the world community successfully, never done before. Unprecedented is the only apt word to describe the happenings. And then, this. India is truly living through historic changes. This is a moment in history which will change the destiny of the nation. For sheer chutzpah, there is no equivalent.

In India the numbers are big. BIG. When you can handle these numbers – for example the several rescue missions spearheaded by the inimitable VK Singh, who is credited with coining the much used term 'Presstitute' (I don't know if this has been included in the latest Oxford Dic, if not should be done pronto, could be a special edition too), you have arrived. And, to echo RN Tata, you have started to act as a leader and not as a follower.

The DeMo (it even rhymes with TaMo, its predecessor event) event cannot be understood by many – a majority – of Indians because we are used to thinking small. In my classes I often say that Indian companies don't know what is big. The largest of them had a turnover of some 400,000 crores at its peak (some 60 billion USD) with a single site operation essentially, whereas the global big ones are more like 550 Billion USD. So far India and Indians have remained pygmies, with their thinking caps able to accommodate only up to 60 Billion USD. But then Modi is cut from a different cloth. He thinks Big. In Jim Collins' words, BHAGs.

The DeMo effort cannot be fathomed by pygmies – the Press, pappu, Mayawati, Lalu, Mulayam, Mamta et al (a galaxy of corrupt, goonda oriented, riff raff) of the opposition. The only exception is the self-proclaimed IITan (I refuse to acknowledge that I am also one) Kujliwal who has shown his true colours, out politicking even the hardest of the dyed in the cloth Indian pol. Even Lalu has shown some restraint, refusing to tow the ill –advised gimmicky Mamta bandwagon. He gave 'outside support'.

That the Press did not have an inkling of the DeMo from NaMo speaks volumes. The NDTV needs to hang its head in shame and Barkha Dutt should stick to conducting small shows like 'The Buck Stops Here' (and will never go anywhere).

Of course, many economists are adding to the clamour., trying to understand the impact, the effects, the long term advesarials etc from a here-and-now point of view. Lots of words but little demonstration of wisdom and little understanding that a new India is emerging. One that will bring back the old glory that this land is famous for. For which the British, the Dutch, Danes, the Portuguese, the Pharsees, the Arabs, the Chinese, the Jews and everyone else yearned to get to know and find 'ashray' in. I don't think any conventional Indian brought up on the western oriented English education can even fathom how the country is changing.

This is only the trailer, we are in for a rollicking time, put on your seat belts and buckle up. The sky is the limit. Thamaso Maa Jyothir Gamaya.

---

## India should chart a new path

In the words of the Mahatma India lives in its villages. This is as true of the India of his times as now. Close to 50% of the world's population lives in rural areas. Two thirds of India is rural. So, it seems that villages will continue to be important demographic centres of action.

Modern societies seem to gravitate to urban living. Even in China almost 60% of the population lives in urban areas. This is a scourge. Nothing exemplifies a monolithic approach to living as much as urbanisation. That so many people will live closely huddled while a whole lot of sunshine and rain fall in rural areas is a pathetic commentary on the role of capitalism in economic development. Instead of spreading wealth capitalism seems to want to centralise development with the urban dominating the rural. As long as this is so the migration and emptying of rural areas will continue and the resultant unhealthy living will only fill the pockets of doctors.

Living for a standard of living seems to be the mantra of developed economies. Led by the USA developed countries have, with a vengeance, lived for economic growth. Never mind the concentration of wealth in a few hands, the vast population migrations uprooting millions of people from an environmentally friendly way of living to a TV & movie addicted, auto mobiled way of life. When was the last time you heard about the movements of the mohalla crow who used to perch on your window sill?

Modern societies are great creators of wealth, but the enabling processes are environmentally destructive in the long run, people unfriendly in the short run. The monotheistic way of pursuing wealth at any cost and to the exclusion of other worldly engagements has led to an engine which consumes coal and belches out smoke, and not a sleek, smokeless jet engine which propels a mass of people towards a bright future.

India has the capacity to change all this. We have the opportunity to create wealth in a way that no one has done so far. Can we make villages wealth creators? 3 D printing seems to be the answer. Industry 4.0 is a part of the answer. Internet of Things (IOT) is right up there. Smart cities are the new fulcrums of localised prosperity in a shared-values world which will spread wealth at the point where it is created, instead of the current model where the wealth creators are few and the recipients are some, many being left out. Imagine a new world where small factories are producing goods to meet local demands. Goods don't need to be transported over long distances. Everyone buys what he wants and not what others are buying (in an urban setting this 'be as thy neighbour' syndrome gets to extremes) and with e Commerce anyone can buy from anywhere.

E Commerce is a great leveller. It has eliminated or minimised the need to maintain large inventories. A e Commerce retailer can source the ordered goods from anywhere and hence the place where the goods are available will get the orders. And over a period of time everyone will get an opportunity to fulfil orders. Which means village level small goods manufacturing entities serving needs in rotation.

India seems to have rushed into the services industry phase in preference to manufacturing. The dependence of a large part of the population on agriculture has deprived the country of skilled hands to man positions in industry. Over the last 20 years + there has been a decline in the agri sector, however, it appears that the workforce released from agri has not entered the manufacturing sector but perhaps the services sector has benefited, IT included.

Historically India has been good at trade and soft skills. It appears that this trend is continuing and will be greatly useful in creating an IOT dependent, industry 4.0 driven economy which will be decentralised, shorn of large organised companies with huge factories, with some exceptions, and, through the smart cities route create a new model for economic development which will be ecofriendly and not uproot the ancient roots of life styles which were more sustaining and sustainable.

# Chapter 9

# Only for You

### The new steel bridge

A bridge too far, or too costly, as per your view. This is the newest news amongst the many ones that is grabbing eyeballs about Karnataka driven events in the national press. I too blinked for a minute. A steel bridge? Gimme a break.

For an untrained eye imagining a steel bridge is a stretch. How would it look? Would it be dark in colour or painted pink? Will it be heavy or light with some cotton and nylon thrust in between steel girders? This is a deadly coup by the innovative and bold Siddy, the CM of Karnataka. For one thing, one must admire the way that Sid has managed the Cauvery issue, although, in one sense he has done great long-term damage to the rule of law in the land by boldly defying the SC order. But the cunning man that he is has manoeuvred in such a way that even the BJP had to attend the all-party meeting where the resolution to disobey the SC order was taken by the assembly. This clearly shows that there are pockets in the BJP which still have not heard the view from Delhi – that development, and not politicking, is the way forward. It is a great pity that the party led by Modi and Amit Shah had to compromise in such a manner. The Cauvery is a deep river indeed. Hope it will wash away such sins.

After manoeuvring the assembly coup of the Cauvery Sid then turned his attention to the steel bridge. This is a novel idea. I am not aware of many such bridges in other parts of the world (no doubt a few are there, which we will come to), other than the one I have seen in old Mumbai chawls where from one building to the other you could walk on such steel 'bridges' made up of a few steel beams anchored precariously at each end. I must say that the idea is bold – and diversionary, a real googly. When the going gets tough, the tough get going!

A lot of people are now left wondering who thought of this piece of modern marvel? Surely Superman will have to be invited to erect the girders, the steel sheets and the lot. The weight of the bridge is hopefully less than the foundation upon which it will have to stand, and knowing Bengaluru roads, one cannot be faulted for entertaining doubts on this score. But if one were to look at the proposal as explained in one of the papers it appears that this steel bridge will go over the proposed concrete flyover which is already under construction at the Hebbal junction. An expert from the IISc is quoted as saying that such a construction i.e. a bridge over another is feasible in view of the metro running over the western expressway in Mumbai! Clearly this expert is no expert as he has not seen the multi layered roads in many American cities. Looks like a scam is brewing.

Steel bridges are not new to the world or India. The Howrah bridge, the legend from Kolkata, is one of the most lovable of such bridges. It is used by millions of people and has withstood the vagaries of the weather, various governments, people of all hues and birds and beasts. There are others too like the Oakland bridge in LA which is nearly all steel. But one is not clear why the fuss? No doubt, my old company Tata Steel could benefit, if, like the British armoured cars in WW II, they could supply this steel also. But then the plan released by the BDA – Bangalore Development Authority – smells, to put it politely. One flyover is already on at Hebbal and this steel bridge will be a split dual carriageway construction, on both sides of the Hebbal flyover, at a height of about 11 to 12 metres. Hairbrained, to say the least. But then engineers can always to make such things. But why should a government lay one flyover over another and then waste money, steel, concrete and jam up the space? As I said before, no one can blame you if you blame the government of hatching up another scam in the true congress way. Way to go, Sid.

## Change in SPJIMR – the Book Reviews Presentations by the Faculty!

Trust the Dean of the SPJIMR to come out with a very interesting idea. He asked all of us hardworking professors to study a book and make a presentation on what we learnt. Not a bad idea, but, initially, many of us may have felt that he is not helping us at all, what with the burden of carrying the academic and non-academic workload. But, at the end of the presentations, one understood the power of the idea and the overall learning, which was equivalent to several months of reading. Let us see how this is an out of the box idea.

The fact that as many as nine leading, currently relevant books were selected was significant – imagine how someone would have had to spend a lot of time going over many titles before justifying to oneself the selection, especially to a group of professors which thinks the world of itself, knowledge-wise! And then the learned professors were asked to volunteer to pick a book to read. Some might say this is a risky thing to do. However, to everyone's surprise the books were grabbed quickly by an eager group, which appeared to be raring to go.

How did this come about? Perhaps the last several months of work has changed the attitude of the group, to volunteer, although one might still wish that more had volunteered! There are no limits! Kotter defines eight principles for transformation of an organisation. In SPJIMR, I think we have absorbed the principles quite well. Kotter would be proud!

Evidently democracy has its uses. To inculcate a spirit of involvement and engagement from an institution, in which strong cultural and established traditions have taken firm roots, into new areas of endeavour is a classic case for Kotterism. Another organisational transformation which we undertook in Tata Steel many years back, albeit on a much larger canvas, comes to mind. Our then MD Dr. Jamshed Irani termed the effort 'Turning the Titanic'. He was inspired by Louis Gerstner's 'Elephants Can Dance' effort in IBM. And in SPJIMR we had a cataclysmic event last year when the much-revered Dean Dr. Manesh Shrikant left us all in splendid isolation, after accomplishing so much. His was a hard act to follow. To take up a major revamp so soon after the 'SPQuake' calls for guts, with no buts.

But we have found the ideal foil in the new Dean who has ideated and energised a faculty team used to Dr. Shrikant's administrative style. The last year has been full of new ideas to give a new direction to the Institute. Research, Design Thinking, Women's Leadership, an Incubation Centre for start-ups, and so on. To top it all we have now re-imagined the flagship event the SBAC, which has been a defining dimension of the SPJIMR – industry interface for some years now. To kick off the re-imagination the 'out of the box' idea of laying a logical, well thought out, innovative foundation was revealed some weeks before. It was mentioned several times to test out the 'waters", so to say, if the faculty would 'bite". Bite it did and how! Today the culminating part was played out in the Faculty Lounge. I am sure that with this exciting beginning we will soon see follow up actions leading to a great SBAC. We are on a roll.

---

## The power of advertising

I saw the TOI online today and my eyes almost popped out. Netizens, especially those with a funny bone, are seemingly getting naughty and imaginative. How else can you explain this ad in the Mocktail section. A dashing, oldish, cowboy type with a dabba of pan bahar! The moustache is classic Delhiwali, the suit is undoubtedly Raymonds, the style of holding the dabba is Gabbarish, the face – of Pierce Brosnan. Of the Bond, James Bond infamy. The video, I believe, features Pierce, with a piercing stare at the dabba, followed by a slam dunk of a 'Kolkata Masala' in his mouth, and spitting out the red stuff through the left end of his mouth, amidst a set of clenched teeth. Lalu could learn something from this stylish, new way to promote not only pan but spitting it out as well.

The way to promote products through advertisements is ages old. The first perhaps was the one featuring Lord Ganesh and Ved Vyasa, with a copy of the Mahabharata displayed in the background, with a blurb, 'sitting cross legged is cool, you can write one lakh lines and more. Try it out, you will never need yoga'. The main theme of this ad is health (most appropriate for our times, and hence of public interest), the key actors are both giants in their own ways but both needing some help in the health area, and their co-produced product is one of the longest running storylines in any part of the world. And, to cap it all, the focus is on 'health for anyone, anywhere, anytime". And the reference to yoga is politically correct for the times we live in. So just imagine what impact this ad will have on the Indian public waiting for new ideas.

The power of an ad is in its characters, those with whom the public can identify. Ganesha is one such personality who blends himself into any number of scenarios, any landscape. You can see him in the streets of Indonesia, in Singapore, In Malaysia, in Pakistan, in Afghanistan, in the USA. Anyone can draw him, just like the line sketch of Gandhiji. He is unique, the only elephant in the world with a human body.

If the public jells with the character, then the ad is a hit. Such favourites are Amitabh Bachchan, Rajnikant, Narendra Modi, Pappu, Kejriwal, Lalu. However, the overall character of an ad is not the sum of the charisma of the characters in it, it is the idea that counts. As Boeing says, quantity, we can count, but quality we can count on. So, one must energise the pep of an ad through a message, subtle imagery, populated by well-known characters with whom the audience can empathise and thus synergise the whole piece. Into this scene we now have Pierce Brosnan, with a pan to boot.

An ad also needs to be current although the characters may be aged, not in the sense of elderly, but in terms of the time period they graced the public. Let me clarify. Mahatma Gandhi may be old in terms of the period that he trod this earth, but his relevance is still very much felt. One more aspect of an ad – it needs to be classy. Which is to say, colours which bounce off light, characters who are loud and crude (dada Kondke, did you say), messages bad in language (like the dalaali of blood or mauth ka saudagar) do not a great ad make. In fact, they actively interfere and also take away from it.

So, the next time you want to come up with a good ad, do read the Mocktail reports of the TOI and other papers too. That will enrich our ads and also tickle the funny bone, we need this nowadays especially after the aftermath of the surgical strikes.

## Terrorism in the modern-day world

Armed terrorism causing destruction to life and property has been in vogue for some time now in parts of the world. The only saving grace is that the expression ‘parts of the world’ can still be used. This is because the area of terror is just now confined to the favourite places – Afghanistan, India, Iraq, Turkey, Pakistan, USA. Some other places like UK, Myanmar, Philippines, Thailand, Ireland keep moving in and out of the terror map – fortunately for them. France is the latest addition, and the severity may reach the proportions seen in Iraq if not tackled in time and in an appropriate manner. Current efforts seem to indicate that the French lack the expertise to deal with this monster which is encircling the nation. Belgium is also in the same boat. They could learn from the Philippines, Myanmar and Thailand which seem to have put a temporary stop to all locally engendered terrorism.

The IS is only a new entrant in the continuum of agencies and movements which have been entering the arena of terrorism. There have been others – the IRA, the Spanish, the Shining Path and other guerrillas in South America, the al Qaeda, the JEM /JUD and other movements in Pakistan. Each one of these agencies has an agenda to oppose some cause and establish its own cause by non-peaceful means. This very methodology clearly indicates that civil society does not accept their view points. This is the cause of the friction. Which often leads to conflict, bloodshed and violence. These groups appear to have never heard of Mahatma Gandhi, the Frontier Gandhi, Martin Luther King and Nelson Mandela. It appears that Sri Sri made an attempt to speak with IS and al Qaeda and was immediately rebuffed so severely that he had to beat a hasty retreat.

Given this background what is the way forward to deal with the mayhem and killings that are bound to happen in the near future? One, do not panic. Looking at the media reportage one might get an impression that the terrorists have gained the upper hand and occupied a lot of territory. Far from it. Even as of now terrorism remains a small-scale activity which can be handled by the police and, in extreme cases, the military.

However, what is disheartening is that hardly any effort is being made to engage with the terrorists in a non-violent manner. All terrorists, in the long run, are amenable to reason and logic. There is no historical parallel that any new country has been created through terrorism. Unless the mass of people supports the new movement – which then becomes a revolution, initiative for change etc – the terrorists will find themselves isolated, sooner or later.

In the present case one must find the forces for peace. They are there – Saudi Arabia, Iran, Turkey, Egypt – which all must pool in to control and, over the long term, arrive at some tolerable level of equilibrium. In the case of India and Pakistan India has been doing a good job of containing the terrorist forces, while taking some casualties. The news yesterday mentioned a figure of 709 such casualties over the entire period, which is not bad considering the carnage in Iraq and the 9 /11. One should accept some casualties as the price to be paid in the short term – and short term has to be defined flexibly - to deal with misguided and violent forces who espouse the bullet over the pallet (of the entire spectrum of life in its splendid variety).

In all cases where the containment has been done the local countries involved themselves took the lead and finally overcame the terrorists and got them to lay down their arms. In the current case the IS should be contained by Iran, Iraq and the other countries named before, with the support of some nearby countries who have the political systems to deal with negotiations. Another thought is to form a Coalition for Peace which will deal with the specific issues of terrorism only. This body must be entitled to negotiate with those who sponsor terrorism and get them around. With all the developments that have taken place in honing the human mind this should not be a big problem. Let's do it.

## Corporates run Mumbai Hospitals now!

What is happening to the dull and drab hospital scene in Mumbai? Of late I find that many doctors who, only the other day, were finding it difficult to snare customers, are now attending conferences funded by others, charging Rs. 500 per visit, mostly to tell you to go and get a battery of tests done (because hospitals have imported many high-tech gadgets, and if these are not used frequently, then what will happen to them?). Hospitals are springing up in the unlikeliest of places – in shopping complexes (no doubt to take care of patients whose hearts are adversely affected after they see their bills), near police stations (to ensure that the 'torture in custody' cases are attended to immediately), next to large housing complexes and even right next to slums. Looks like hospitals are getting braver by the day and are not averse to residing cheek by jowl near unhygienic and disease prevalent places. They want to be close to their customers.

Like in all things in India hospitals are also finding their spot in the sun. Many specialists are returning to India, as also many are going out too, especially after a great education from Bihar, to attend to the increasing demand by the local populace to seek and remedy the many ills that society is inflicting on them and vice versa. Just look at the corporate acquisitions. Fortis is out to take out the rigor mortis from financially weak private hospitals by acquiring many of them, Apollo has gone solo to build, Reliance is relying more and more on the hospital business to shore up the 'sick' companies that are getting accumulated, and so on.

The scene, once ruled by the Hinduja, the Jaslok, the venerable Nanavati, Raheja, Sushrut, the KEM, the Cooper hospital (there is not one day in Mumbai when this hospital is not mentioned in the dailies) (the saying goes that Cooper is for those who have really decided to sever their ties with the world) is now increasingly coming under attack by corporates. In the good old days, some well-meaning citizens-built hospitals to provide succour to the needy. They ran the show pretty much like a family business, with a temple in the premises and various Gods and Goddesses being propitiated every day to ensure the wellbeing of all those who passed through their corridors. The typical Mumbai patient felt a sense of reassurance that their health will be looked after and their pockets will still be in their places after the discharge from the hospital.

Little did the gullible Mumbaikar expect the new era that has dawned. Hospitals are now looking spick and span with steel and chrome fittings, beds and rooms have acquired a new look, with a 'super deluxe' and 'corporate suite' rooms at the top end to lure the HNI's (much like the way banks are looking at these guys), with 'teams' of 'associates' attending each patient (under the thinking that many cooks can make a better broth) and bills that are more driven by the fact whether you are covered by medical insurance or not (that's a subject of another story). To balance this, hospitals declare a part of their facilities available for use to poorer sections of society – thanks to government requirements - where the rates charged are much lower than the loot that goes in the deluxe suites. CEO's and COO's are ruling the roost, with administrative assistants from the latest MBA schools.

In many hospitals the hygiene has taken a turn for the good. Only the other day I went into a small hospital and found that in front of every room they have hung a plastic bottle containing a sanitiser which can be used by the patients and their relatives. Every once a in a while a sweeper comes in to swipe the floor with a well-designed broom. Both dry and wet cleaning are done periodically. It is a welcome change indeed to Mumbaikars who often have to see overfilled garbage containers at the end of every road. Security is now a big thing in many hospitals and one is greeted by a stern looking guard who sometimes also functions as a messenger or compounder. Floors are clean and neat and interiors of hospitals are now comparable to the best 5-star hotels.

In a major change food is now prepared and served in most hospitals, and patients are asked not to bring anything from home. So much so that even relatives eat at the hospital canteen. Mumbai hospitals have sensed that the Aam Mumbaikar is keen to have some upgraded service for which he is even willing to pay, and they are speedily catching up with the market expectations. Jai Mumbai.

## Chapter 10

# In the Arena of Politics and Commerce

**What's with the politicians of this country? And other larger issues**

Recently news reports are full of politicians indulging in non-political shenanigans, of the sexual variety. Not a day passes without some reports on this topic. It is par for the course for such news about politicians from UP and Bihar where the political class is assumed to be capable of such acts, given the level of transactions in the public domain. However, for the national capital to be bombarded with such news, especially highlighting the role of AAP pols, a party which was voted in with a huge majority, is disturbing, to say the least. All such news nowadays is known in almost all corners of the country, if not the world, over time, instantaneously. Sleaze sells and contributes to TRP's.

No doubt Kejriwal and company is up against the wall with regularity, and, to escape some of this unwanted attention, the Delhi CM is going away to Bangalore for a throat surgery. I strongly suspect that he goes there to meet with Sri Sri, to recharge his political and moral compass. Not that Bangalore is any better, what with land grabs, white water lakes, Cauvery water sharing et al.

It is a moot point what came first – whether the corrupt politician or a bribe giving public which cannot wait to get things. Even if the things that they want are not 'right", some of us go to any lengths to get what we want, bribe or no bribe. While this issue can be debated with spirited participation from both sides, let's look at the pros and cons.

Taking bribes is as old as the hills notwithstanding the contra views from the western world, led by the US. US political history is full of incidents which illustrate that any means can justify the ends. Whose ends will determine the transactional details. Giving bribe to get something done is part of a live and let live culture. Imagine what God would do if 10 % of the world, which is some 600 million bhakts, petition to him every day seeking his intervention. Who will he assist first? There must be some consideration. Bribe is but one of them. There are others, like devotion, dedication, good deeds. Thus, one may argue that bribe is as legitimate a tool in the general toolkit for divine attention. Only it is a tool most favoured by the rich.

Wise politicians know that larger the business, larger the moolah. For example, take India and the US. If the Indian business pays 1 % of its earnings for favours, then the pols earn something in the region of 12 billion USD per year, based on a 2.3 trillion GDP economy. However, the same works out to about 85 billion USD for US pols, where the total number of pols sharing this booty is perhaps less than 50 % of India. This means that per capita, the earnings of pols from considerations in India is some 15 times less. Indian pols should realise that if they allow more businesses to flourish their cut percentage can come down, and, over a larger base, they can become rich faster and earn more too. I wonder what would happen in India the moment the Indian pols realise this simple arithmetic. Had this been known in the licence and permit raj days, no politician would have refused licences. Much like the governments auctioning telecom spectrum every year, getting rich bigtime. Although because of the transparency and online, open auctions, individuals have not been able to take their cuts.

Having established a commercial basis for bribe giving and taking, one can attempt a case that, in the early stages of an economy, poverty is shared, and thus bribing is endemic. However, as the economy grows the argument loses value as wealth is to be shared. But this is not so with the current pastime of Indian pols which is apparently in a different field – sex.

The TOI. from time to time, keeps publishing extracts from the Indian classic 'Bhagavatam", in its 'Spirituality' column, which talks about developments in the Kaliyuga. And the emphasis is on gradual but complete domination of this particular proclivity over all other, even money. The Bhagavatam says that in Kaliyuga a Brahmin will be known only by the fact that he wears the 'sacred thread'. Else he will be no different from any other person in terms of conduct and character. All affairs will be money driven. Sex will be a predominant feature of the society. Reminds one of the last days of Rome and Caligula Caesar.

It appears that Indian pols have taken to heart the Bhagavatam and intend to introduce the forecasts as soon as they can. It is hoped that wiser counsel will prevail and all political parties will be more vigilant in selecting their members. After all the well-known Indian saying is 'Yatha Raaja, Thathaa Prajaa'.

---

## The Gujarat election campaign and its aftermath

If you have nothing to do, please do it in front of your TV, it cannot talk back. On the contrary, you have the option to surf, switch, increase the volume, and, horror of horrors, even happen across Netflix. No hard feelings Netflix, just silly conversation.

And if, in the past few days, you have been doing what I have written above, your ears may have been adversely affected by the recently talked about Canal Dehiscence Syndrome, eyes may have contracted electionovitis, legs may have become inactive due to TVlysis and hands could be feeling the pinch of the TV remote buttons. Nevertheless, you could not have missed the quintessential Indian pastime - elections. With 29 states, one upper house (whose status may be lowered to oblivion), and one lower house at the central level, India is a psephologist's and Pollsters' delight, notwithstanding what Tejaswi Yadav pointed out in today's tweet about the exit poll predictions made for the last Bihar elections. If, in between campaigning for all these elections, you do find the time to implement GST and DeMo, you are not man, you are God. Reminds me of the story about the Russian delegation which visited India during Pandit Nehru's time, and, after a few days, became convinced that there has to be a God. Their reasoning – how else could an entity called India exist and thrive? They immediately cancelled their membership from the communist party, apocryphally, just like our own Mani from Mayiladuthurai.

Getting back to the Gujarat elections, the most talked about item was the 'LOW standards that were visible throughout the electioneering' (capitals used for emphasis). The learned members of the TV press expressed their complete abhorrence and disapproval, unsolicited, of course, of the shenanigans resorted to by one and all, especially the non-vikas related banter, chatter and chana chapattar. Commentator after panellist, continuously, and in strong terms, denounced the 'unparliamentary' language used. This term refers to the language, presumably, to the one used in the mecca of democracy, because, there is considerable evidence that the language used in Indian houses of legislatures, is, often, something else.

What began, innocently enough, as a debate between civil people, on the vikas of Gujarat and the now-known-to-even-a-two-year-old-child 'Gujarat Model", very soon crashed into the deep middle of the Sabarmati, with a big thud, and quagmired into the deep sand pits of vulgar language, vociferous repartee, irrelevant cacophony, high decibel rhetoric and 'Gujarati Manoos' jingoism.

There are some lessons here. The election was more of a war than a friendly confrontation, which is the way it usually is, in the marketplace of Indian democracy, as per past practice. The high ego level of the Indian intellect comes into prominence in the field of untempered and unmoderated election propaganda. This is a field where agriculture is not practiced, but, instead, weapons of demagoguery are sharpened through actual use.

And when this happens, the spectator is subjected to optical and hearing related imagery which may not always be palatable to the fine tastes.

Second, the issue highlighted by some panellists was – did the BJP not have anything else to concentrate on except Rahul Gandhi? Perhaps, what they meant was that BJP should have spoken about Mamta Banerjee, Derek Obrien, Amrinder Singh and other such – they were feeling left out.

Third, what is the big deal if Rahul Gandhi visits a few temples (something like 50 of them in 2 days). Indians are pious (this gem was actually uttered by a Congress Panellist), they are very God fearing (God fears the Indian is a better description of the actual situation), Hinduism is not a religion, it is not even an 'ism' (this one is OK), and Rahul wears the janevu (this is a bit far-fetched, however, in the great literary creation called 'Bhagavatam' by Sri Narayana Bhattadhri, it is written that, in the Kaliyuga, anyone who wears a janevu will be called a brahmin, and that will be the only identify of the brahmin), and so on. Amidst all this, it was forgotten that, what Rahul does, and whatever he does, is open to scrutiny, this is elections season, and, so far, the Election Commission has not yet banned this.

Fourth, the word 'vikas' went out of the window (or whatever else), after the second or the third day. One should be thankful that it was used to open the innings, and spin was not introduced in the opening over itself.

What do these happening convey? For me, it shows that the world may be changing, but somethings stay the same. One such is war. One is reminded of the Mahabharata war. In Indian writings of yore, popularly known as 'shastras", the rules of war have been codified. These were used (intended to be used is more appropriate) in the 18-day Mother of all Wars – the Mahabharata war at Kurukshetra. Sample some of the rules. One, war must be waged ONLY between the armies, no civilian involvement, no civilian atrocities to be committed, like, rape, pillaging and plunder. Obviously, neither Mahmud of Ghazni nor Alauddin Khilji were aware of these rules, neither, for that matter, was Hitler. Two, war should be fought between EQUALS ONLY, i.e., horsemen should fight horsemen, elephant rider should fight with another, men with swords should only fight with those with swords. In the new age war, everyone hides, and a bomb or a bullet does not distinguish based on caste or profession. Three, men specially trained in verbally abusing the enemy, should fight only with those on the other side who also do the same. Just imagine, in modern times, abuses are so common, and the use of four-letter words are so frequent, that one wonders how the 'abuser only' rule was even formulated in the ancient times. Four, war should start ONLY after SUNRISE, at a fixed time agreed to both parties, and should STOP at the pre-fixed, agreed upon time. Beyond those hours, armies were expected to visit each other, and help each other to recover from the day's damages. No modern equivalent, barring the few stories of bravery and compassion of individual soldiers. There were more such rules which governed warfare in ancient India. Foreign invaders who raided India were used to an altogether different way of fighting, that included plunder, rape, himsa and destruction. Obviously, Indian kings stood no chance.

When the Mahabharata war began, rules were obeyed, openers were clear on what was to be done, etc, but, from the second day onwards, in the heat of the battle, more and more rules were violated. The FINAL DENOUEMENT came when Ashwatthama killed the sons of the Pandavas in a dastardly mid night attack of treachery and treason, unimaginable even to those warriors who had witnessed the horrors of war till that night.

In Kaliyuga, the nature of the human being is such that, rules will be flouted, more rules will be cast aside and all hell will break loose, given a chance. That is what happened in Gujarat. Let us all make a note, make amends where possible, take lessons for the future, but be aware that this is Kaliyuga.

**DeMo – towards a new India**

## What's going on?

Looking at the rash of news coverage over DeMo one might get an impression that the PM has a great grudge against India, that he is out to make India poor instead of Make in India. From the 'learned' to the opposition to the every-one except the common man seems to have taken the PM's actions somewhat personally, taking out their frustration of whatever is frustrating everyone. No one, it appears, is willing to look at the long term, willing to admit that India needs to change, that 'chalta hai' has to make a move and the jugaad era has to end. To be replaced by refinement in speech, behaviour, thinking, living and seeking moksha.

Let's look at the most common refrains. The PM did not consult the 'learned' economists and other relevant babus.

This is a just a factitious comment, the PM has set up the Niti Aayog, he has access to several economists including Amartya Sen, he has had interactions with Raghuram Rajan, Arvind Subramaniam, Panagariya and others. Now if these are not eminent economists then they must be hiding somewhere. So much about 'not consulting economists".

The PM didn't give enough time. Sure, he didn't. His idea was to get them by surprise. Surprise? Tell me another thing. People forget that he got elected on a platform where he promised to get after black money. In the usual Indian way people thought that he is carrying forward the tradition of chalta hai and hence not to be taken seriously. Innumerable schemes have been announced since the time he took over as the PM and several warnings have been issued to black money holders to come clean. Those who are now carping have conveniently chosen to ignore all these. Myopic is a mild word. Deliberate forgetfulness? Support for the unsupportable? Or simply trying to stay relevant?

People have died standing in queue for money. True, to some extent. But to what extent? No doubt these are regrettable but at the time of independence there were thousands of people who voluntarily gave up gold, jewellery, their lives on being asked to do so by Mahatma Gandhi. The descendants of these same people are today willing to undergo some difficulties so that the nation can get a new direction. Indians are not new to sacrifices. The common Indian is made of a different stuff than the western educated, Keynes quoting, capitalistic leaning 'thinkers".

It is shocking that a section of the opposition has done its best to make things difficult for the government – and the people at large. The common Indian will never forgive the frenetic, fanatical opposition parties, having gotten to where they currently are through ill gotten money, corrupt practices, communal shenanigans (the Didi stands out in this regard), and their total disregard for the common man's situation. The congress wants the poor to stay poor forever so that they can get votes. I am unable to understand the Didi and their ilk, who, in spite of a rich cultural heritage, are unable to fathom a populace which can earn and live life happily instead of being mired in poverty through generations. Is there something to be admired in being poor? Is it something for which one must fight for? Isn't it time we did something to alleviate poverty and take it out of the electoral equation?

## So, what's has been missed?

In all this hullaballoo the forest has been missed by barking up the wrong trees. India needs to move, there must be wealth creation to abolish poverty forever. We don't want the situation where millions of Indians are not able to live a decent life, whereas their brethren in other countries seem to be enjoying themselves. The PM is the only person who has made developmental economics his electoral plank, and, in spite of being from a humble background, he is aware of what to do than the many theory spewing pundits who have only kept this country backward and poverty stricken. The concern over the dip in economy in the short term is a totally misplaced, myopic view of the movement that the PM has just kicked off. The long term will prove that the right path has been shown and we need to travel that way.

The larger message from the PM is: India is changing. This has been in evidence ever since he became the PM. The usually apologetic, cringing, servile, western thought dominated Indian is now ultimately standing up. The diplomatic blitzkrieg, the sharp increase in the perception of the world over India's role in the future world (now, don't start the same old routine – where is the evidence, it is all in the mind), the winning ways of many of our sportspersons, the overall sense of optimism that is prevailing in the country (there are some exceptions to this, those who will not let the country forget that it is poor and that that is the only way to continue) are visible to all those who want to see.

The entire populace has given a resounding yes to the PM's actions. This is a stupendous achievement. It is heartening that, from the perception that India is a nation of cheats, where it is impossible to root out corruption and thirdrateness, we are moving towards a transparent, vibrant, connected, corruption free, efficient country. Where else in the world will you find a poor populace willing to put up with hardships to usher in a new society? Where else will you find a nation of poor people willing to stand in queues and still support the actions of a determined government willing to provide leadership towards a greater India?

All those who are against the current movement will be left out. They have missed the one biggest ingredient for change – the readiness, willingness, receptivity of those who have to bear the brunt of the change. Kotter will be delighted.

The people have spoken, hope all will listen.

# Chapter 11

# Management

**What effect will the GST have on business?**

After a lot of political manoeuvring and chest thumping the GST has seen the light of the hoary halls of the parliament. In fact, the run has been so fast that the President has already signed the bill before anyone could say 'Timbuktu". One is reminded of the popular Rajnikant joke, that he came first as usual, but Einstein was stunned that light came in second!

GST has gotten into India after many years of VAT. Another milestone in the tax structure. In the days after independence there was a great fear that businessmen will enrich themselves at the expense of the country if left free, and so, many layers of safeguards were built around their activities. Those who did all this didn't reckon that these self-same safeguards will give rise to another monster – the corrupt politician. Unfortunately, the political class will find it difficult to live down this reputation. It will take many years before the country will even begin to forget the illegalities, the continuous cheatings, the back stabbings and small-minded thinking that this licence and permit raj brought about in its wake.

In all the actions after independence this one aspect of the nation's business development is perhaps the most painful one, and the costliest mistake. It is a carryover of the 'lack of self-respect' of the Hindu that Subramanian Swamy, Rajiv Malhotra and others of their class talk about – we lacked the vision that the opening up of industry will usher in an era of prosperity instead of one that would lead / continue the exploitation. Experts and pundits will keep debating whether this was the right way to go, but the political leadership of those early years believed more in the negative effects than in the beneficial ones of business.

Now that the GST has become a reality the business world in India needs to redeem itself and chart a new path of development, wealth creation and equitable distribution, sustainable growth and world class quality. The challenges confronting the Indian business community are far more multifarious than ever before. Just imagine, the western business world has had an uninterrupted run of free enterprise over the last one hundred years which has seen unbridled growth without the fetters of sustainability, conservation, environmental pollution and so on. These new factors, which are the results of the damages done by the huge consumption and growth, and which have made the cost of doing business a lot more than what it was before, have started affecting adversely the cost of doing business only in the last ten to fifteen years or so. And now the Indian industry will have to bear the full brunt of this increase.

The GST – consisting of CGST, SGST and IGST - is another attempt to smoothen the myriad tax laws that govern interstate transfer of goods. While the VAT tried to remove the double counting of taxes applicable for sales between companies in creating the final product, the GST will remove the layers of taxes and documentation that need to be done now to get goods across state borders.

Take, for example, a producer in Maharashtra, who wants to sell goods in West Bengal. He has to transfer the goods using a C form which will allow for a tax-free transport to WB. If the C form is not given then the WB state sales tax of about 10 % + will be levied on the CIF value of the goods that leave the Maharashtra factory upon entry into WB. On top of this the CST will become applicable when the goods are sold in WB. So, there is an additional tax element of about 15 % on the FOB value. Now this amount will be subsumed in the GST as IGST and will not be that high, providing some relief. Differential tax rates can be avoided to some extent, based on the rates that are finally decided by the central authority.

States where manufacturing happens will not get any revenue for the materials leaving the state. Earlier they would levy the State Sales tax on such transfers based on which the C form could be raised to avoid tax in the consumption state. Thus, manufacturing states that stand to lose out on tax will be compensated for five years. By then some mechanism will have to be found to remove this inequality.

The fact is that a whole host of central and state taxes – including Central Excise Duty, Additional Excise Duties, Service Tax, Additional Customs Duty (CVD) and VAT / Sales tax, Luxury tax, State Cesses and Surcharges relating to supply of goods and services, Entry tax not in lieu of Octroi – will be subsumed under the GST. The entire mechanism will create a smooth tax collection and a transparent linkage structure, with lower sales tax rates overall, will come as a big relief to all those who are interested in doing business. As they say the GST has now announced to the world that India is ready for business.

## E Commerce (EC) and the new paradigms in Operations Management

There was time when companies used to produce one or two products and sell them in a welcoming market. The Ford Model T comes to mind. Beginning there we have come a long way, baby. In companies like HUL which has a string of brands – I hope the top management is aware of all of these, they multiply and get subtracted and morphed so fast – and, under each brand, there are some 15 to 20 variants. The product mix can be mind boggling. Similarly take a company like Tata Steel. With a hot rolling mill, a cold rolling mill and several rods products mills, the number of products in the product mix could easily exceed a thousand.

To deal with these complexities automation and computer advancements have aided a great deal. Let us look at some of the complexities. First, the number of customers. They have gone up geometrically, as also classified into layers – wholesalers, distributors, stockists, retailers, and, finally, the end customers. Just imagine, your company had 1 product and 100 distributors. And each distributor placed an order once a month and was supplied once a month. This makes for 100 orders and supplies each month, respectively. Now consider, the product mix increases to 1,000. The tiered layer of distributors etc is now a huge 1,000, plus end customers which the company serves directly through company owned dedicated stores. If you include only the tiered layers, then we have 1,000. Let us assume each distributor orders for 50 products every month through 50 orders. Thus, we have now 1,000*50*50 orders per month, or, 2.5 million orders per month! And you haven't even begun to consider the company owned stores. You get the photo.

So, from 100 orders to 2.5 million orders, that's talking. What affect will this have on the manpower requirements? Let's say that you employed one person to handle 100 orders, and that, over time, he could handle 1,000 orders per month, with the help of some automation, SAP etc. Poor sap, he is still stretched. Now consider that the orders have gone up to 2.5 million per month! So how many people will you hire? I leave it to your imagination. You can now appreciate why CEO's salaries have jumped by orders of magnitude, they have to deal with these magnitudinous problems.

Now, multiply by the amazing number that one is seeing on TV screen these days. Amazon is offering 2.5 crore items for sale through the EC. Let me tell you the zeroes – 25,000,000, 25 million. And then today I saw another shocker. eBay is offering 100 million items or 10 crore items on its platforms. Isn't the world going nutty?

Let us look at the impact on logistics. If, for the 100 orders 10 trucks were needed every month, one might be tempted to say that for 2.5 million orders, one might need 250,000 trucks. Making allowance for a compression ratio of 1: 100 the requirement will come down to 2,500. What's going on? What has EC unleashed? Logistics will go loony, transport will go bonkers and roads will be soon flooded by CV (Commercial Vehicles like trucks, pickups, trailers, containerised truck etc) traffic.

But the figures of CV sales show that, in India, over the last few years, the demand has been going down. So, what's happening? With Amazon, Flipkart (let's hope the cart wont flip), Snapdeal and the lot, one would have looked forward to a big boost to CV's. But I guess another phenomenon is hitting the logistics scene – that of smaller vehicles like the Tata Ace, Mahindra Maximo and the tempos. And then the UAV's (of the 'surgical strikes' fame) and the drones. While overall the need for logistics has increased manifold, the log – mix is undergoing a change due to the advent of EC. Most of EC sales is retail and wholesale is perhaps on the decline. This can lead to a reduction in the need for large, tonnage trucks, but smaller trucklets, with shorter run spans.

And then the number of orders – this is the biggest paradigm changer. Whereas materials managers and procurement specialists dealt with 'reasonable' numbers of items, the explosion of offers from the likes of Walmart, Safeway, Amazon, Flipkart, Snapdeal and their ilk is likely to cross 'reasonable' limits by large margins. This will surely lead to changes in purchase practices, materials receipts, storage practices, warehousing and warehouse practices, monitoring of stocks systems (I think RFID will soon, if not already, have to make way for something else). This indicates that the future tasks, skill sets, competencies required of personnel in company employment will be quite different. Digital systems will have to be used in much larger areas and in a much more intensive manner. Linked, interactive, AI inbuilt systems will have to be the norm rather than the exception. Software will have to be everywhere.

Welcome to the brave new world of Operations Management – whose name itself will have to change to Value Stream Management. This is a world where systems are studied in a holistic and integrated manner, without the classical finance, HR, operations etc. Value Streams will deliver values to customers through a seamless network of linked and interactive series of systems, to drive which one needs multiple, cross functional knowledge and expertise. So, the future world will be one of higher specialisation, but more broad-based knowledge coverage. That's the brave new world of Value Driven Society.

## The industrial world – and what it implies

Even in his wildest dreams would James Watt have never known what he had wrought in 1761. By inventing and patenting the steam engine he had let loose the monster called 'industrial revolution' into an unsuspecting world. The rolling that he started gathered a huge momentum when Henry Ford assembled his famous assembly line and circulated himself to fame and fortune. The invention of the computer sealed the fate of all things non-industrial, making industry the only and the most important prime mover of economic growth.

To the extent that one starts suspecting whether one is living and consuming endlessly to keep the standard of living high! We are told, the more the consumption, the better the standard of living. The math is very simple. Mass production brings costs down, but what one is not told is that mass production can work only when supported by mass consumption. So, the leaders who espouse mass production as the panacea for all social ills always look out form the corner of their eyes to check and ensure that someone is convincing everyone to consume – anything and everything. No wonder General Electric is reputed to have sent a sales team to sell refrigerators to eskimos.

The word ‘modern’ can be used today for anything and everything which supports an industrial way of life. Be it music, be it the arts, be it handicrafts. If it aint financially lucrative, it aint nothing. Money is the logical corollary to the mass production concept. Mass earnings. Mass money follows mass scale. Like in Berkshire Hathaway and Warren Buffett, and George Soros and Mukesh Ambani.

Everything is measured by its ‘mass”. As in democracy. It is the quantity that you have to count on. A wit remarked ‘quantity can be counted, but one can ONLY count ON quality’. Without quality, quantity cannot count. Only discount. In classical supply chain management terms – quantity discount!

The pastoral life of the early ages has vanished in many parts of the world, but still manages to hold its position in India.

Even today one can see the cowherd, the potter, the cowshed, the muddy roads, the cattle grazing in the land on which once Krishna played the flute for them. Contrast the two and you get the picture. A world where industry is becoming all prevalent, and money the driver of all human endeavour. As they say, money is not everything. It is the only thing. So is industry.

But it is not as bad as it may appear. The industrial world has its charms. The easy availability of musical programs in any part of the world through the TV and the electronics that back it to anyone, in any part. The end of drudgery with computers and automation taking up primary positions in industrial activities. The coming digital revolution, the IOT, industry 4.0 and the works. Ultimately it is up to man to figure out how to program the Frankenstein's Monster created and let loose by James Watt to make life multi-dimensional and sustainable. The planet will depend on this.

## Quality Management in modern manufacturing

Quality as a word has been changing its dimensions, its applicability, its size, its scope of work, coverage and last, but not the least, its stakeholders. Let's begin tracking this wonderful term on its journey.

I am sure James Watt never spent a waking moment losing sleep over the quality of the steam engine. He may have been far too excited about the very fact of its invention and its far-reaching effects on humanity. Neither did Marconi, Morse, the Curie couple, Sir CV Raman and many other inventors who all contributed to the development of the modern-day industrial society. Nor did Adam Smith, in his tome 'Wealth of Nations' pay much heed to quality. On the contrary Frederick Taylor, in his 'Principles of Scientific Management' went to the extent of studying every minute and every second of what a workman did and how he could be made to work even more, continuously. Little did he spend time on quality. He was, if anything, a 'quantity guru'.

The advent of the Ford assembly line in 1913 enhanced the reputation of engineers who were entrusted with the task of 'mass producing'. This new invention which allowed Ford to produce all colours of cars in black, was the forerunner to the quantity revolution which soon followed. This was because the early days of industrialisation wholly belonged to a 'sellers' market' scenario. And the sellers were milking it for all their worth.

Soon enough, like what Porter later came to say in his 'Competitiveness of Nations' and his 5 forces tool, entry barriers had broken and industry was flooded with many players. They had sensed and felt the lure of profit, and many could make millions if only they had something to sell.

Enter the differentiator – quality. While quality had crept into the industry through 'specifications' which were ensured by armies of inspectors, the entry had been obtained and the age of quality had begun. The 1930's and 1940's saw many champions and pioneers, who sighted 'quality' as the next level, and started their evangelisation. They sang praises of

SQC, management responsibility, team work and management with a human face. There was a rethink on Taylorism and quality gurus like Deming, Juran, Shewhart, Ishikawa, Imaai, Kano, Akao, Crosby preached a new mantra for a new regime of quality. Culminating in TQM in 1950, this movement propelled Japan to the forefront of a global industrial conquest. Soon old behemoths like RCA bit the dust. This went on till the 1980's. This can be called the golden age of quality.

Apart from tools and techniques which mushroomed many thinkers proposed different theories which put to test Taylor and the Hawthorne experiments and inculcated a philosophy of 'integrated' or 'total' management. The effect was that companies discovered that marketing departments need not only consist of people who 'wasted' the company's money by entertaining customers and dealers to ferret out money from customers, but also people who can build brands, increase prices in the most difficult markets and chart new paths through product development to uncharted segments. In the same way accountants discovered their finance side, HR discovered their link to being 'aligned and serving the company's overall operations', and administration, through innovative methods to streamline their activities, found themselves to be 'value adders', just like the production people, who monopolised this title hitherto.

In a sense one could say that companies reinvented themselves in all their full potential and sought to serve customers in many ways thereto unknown or unthought. The prime beneficiary – the customer, who was not only the king, but also the driver of change. The customer became the new stakeholder who made change happen. And this is continuing to this day. May it live long. And he has to thank men like Deming and Toyoda and Ohno who made a different quality happen. But for them we would still be in a sellers' market, with Ford still selling the any colour black car.

## Emerging ecomm businesses and supply chains

Ecommerce is etailing its way into the retail business at great speed. The impact of the ecomm on the retail revolution can be seen in different ways. In short ecomm is likely to become the eway for retail soon, if not already so in many places.

For one, if the ecomm is attached only to the retail business then the effect is that of providing a platform for aggregating demand from multiple customers, from multiple geographies, in one place. This aggregation is the main driver of the low prices which Walmart and others of their ilk promise. Just imagine, the local kirana store can stock some 5 dozen toothpaste tubes, as he caters to a demand of 50 per day in the locality. Hence his ability to offer low prices is limited. If this same seller goes the ecomm way his demand for the toothpaste could go up to 500 or 1,000 per day, and then he can really look at discounted prices. Now you are talking.

The second benefit is the speed with which the sale can be closed. The culture of ecomm fits in well with the overall 'quick' culture of the times. We need quick responses, so we use WhatsApp, never mind that much of WhatsApp is Multiple Forwards and the authenticity is up for questioning. It's like a lie, if repeated several times, becomes truth-like. In an ecomm transaction the customer has implicitly accepted that the goods that he will view will be the ones that he will get – something like WYSIWYG of yore. This predilection of the customer to get what he wants in double quick time works well for ecomm. Abracadabra.

The third benefit is that sales resources need not be deployed to close out a sale. In a big retail store, the other day I saw, at non peak times, it is difficult to make who is the customer and who is the sales person waiting to attend to them. Such confusion can be avoided with ecomm with the concomitant benefit in transaction costs. This may sound harsh in a country where population is considered as an asset, but such is the lure of ecomm.

The fourth is the savings in the non-manpower resources to be used for the sale. For example, for every customer who buys form a ecomm platform and who doesn‘t step into the store, the fuel for the car is saved, the parking lot is available to others, the roads are less subjected to wear and tear, the lights and air-conditioning required to service the store footfalls can be avoided.

The fifth benefit is in the overall lessening of the supply chain resources, especially transport. Consider, if the customers were to come to the store to buy, then the goods have to be transported to the warehouse, thence to the store, from where the customer will cart it to the home. In the ecomm scheme of things, the goods are either in the warehouse or in the kirana stores who partner with the big chains as the fronting delivery teams. In either case one trip is avoided. This is a huge benefit.

Another benefit is that ecomm companies which tend to aggregate demand and sell in large volumes also place large orders with suppliers, who are typically manufacturers. In view of these large orders goods are sold by the manufacturer at lower prices. Barring seasonal goods others are sold through the year and hence this large demand will lead to regular supplies, resulting in stable production runs and the consequent cost and quality benefits. The pull system can be pushed by both buyer and supplier. Warehouses will stock goods in large quantities which then will be handled in bulk, thus speeding up and streamlining unloading and stacking operations. Thus, the overall cost situation is likely to be held in leash and could be one of the reasons why many countries like the USA where such ecomm and retails stores are selling in bulk, inflation remains low.

So, it appears that ecomm is the many splendored thing, like love. Let's enjoy it.

## Cross badging – what are the implications?

The term 'cross badging", or 'badge engineering' entered the lexicon in India sometime in early 2012. Examples are Micra / Pulse, Sunny/Scala, Terrano / Duster (all Nissan / Renault) combos. Similarly, Vento (VW)/ Rapid (Skoda). Tata and Fiat tried to tango, but became untangled soon. Same with Renault and Mahindra. So, why are Maruti and Toyota trying the same failed move again?

The logic is totally unclear. Two cars – with two different names – but looking the same, is one reminded of the ball tampering incidents? Appears like car companies are trying to cheat their customers, trying to take them for a ride, so to say, although that is their USP, when you look at it in the right way. So, where is the catch?

It is common practice that auto majors use the platform strategy to cut down on engineering costs, time to market, advertising and other distribution costs by manufacturing using the same body. However, the names under which these are sold are quite different in different countries. For example, the Qualis, which morphed into the Innova, in India, was sold in Indonesia under the name 'Kijang' for some years, before appearing in India as Qualis. This is a sensible strategy. Make a new car, introduce in a single market, get the learnings, and then roll out in other markets, with localisations, but using the same platform. This works, as, in the case of the Qualis, very few in India knew that the Kijang is the same car, but with a different name. This could be 'not in sight", 'not registered in mind' type of a situation.

The car company is using the fact that, in spite of globalisation, familiarity of customers in different locations, with the several names, is not often high. On the contrary, selling the same car under two or more names in the same location is like using a ten rupee note with different pictures and colours in the same country, which will lead to confusion, counterfeiting and what not.

The platform strategy is useful as a great profit generating engine. In this strategy, one company engineers and produces the basic model. Then, adding bells and whistles, to embellish the base, the company rolls out a full suite of models, to cover a price range. The higher prices charged for the 'higher' level models, makes the profit picture rosy. This has been the strategy used in India and many other countries, by all auto companies, and customers are OK with this, as they understand the logic. For example, one can buy an Omni at a very low price, because it doesn't come with an A/C. Similarly, one is willing to pay up to 4 lakhs for variants of the Maruti Alto, based on the accompaniments. This strategy has the effect of increasing the price tag, disproportionate to the cost increase, and provides a legitimate way to earn an extra rupee, sometimes even to subside the non-profitable low-end models. However, cross badging forms no part of this strategy.

What, then, can be the reasons that Maruti and Toyota are looking at cross badging? The cars being mentioned are Brezza, Baleno and Corolla. It is clear that the companies are trying to build up their coverage of the market. Each one of these vehicles is a successfully selling car. Maruti has a complete coverage of the low end of the market, and is slowly moving up the value chain through Brezza, Baleno, Ciaz and Ertiga. However, this comes at a steep cost – engineering, testing, etc. Also, Maruti does not have any car in the Corolla range, except the Ciaz. Thus, by bringing in the Corolla, Maruti can hopefully speed up its market coverage in the upper, and become the GM of India.

Whereas, Toyota is a niche player, with the Innova being the bulk seller, at about 75,000 per annum. The other best seller is the Fortuner, at about 10,500 last FY. Total Toyota sales for

FY 2017-18 was about 143,000, whereas Maruti was doing 1.7 million. The reach of Maruti is unmatchable, especially in the rural areas. For Toyota to start doing the Maruti volumes will need a hefty investment in the distribution network, apart from the time issue, as well as the range issue. If at all Toyota wants be the number 2 to Maruti, then it needs to have a broader range of models, to cover the lowest to the highest price range. That would be following the lead of GM's Alfred Sloan, who invented the theory of 'a car at every price point". And that can happen by the cross badging.

Maruti has done this quite well in India, with a very strong base, on which it is trying to erect the sedan/MUV/SUV/Luxury segments. The beginning has been successful. However, to give this strategy a kick start, nothing like selling the Corolla, and a few other sedans from the Toyota stable. Maruti is clearly hoping that it can sell 5,000+ Corollas, in addition to the 5,500 Ciaz;s. Toyota will be looking to complement its Etios range with the fully engineered, road tested Brezza and Baleno, to increase its volumes. While Toyota will benefit from the distribution width, Maruti will benefit from the sedan depth. It can avoid the costly engineering that it must have incurred in the Ciaz and Ertiga. No doubt, there is a synergy, unlike any of the earlier cases of cross badging. However, there is a catch.

Every car from a company, develops, over the years, a certain 'vaasna", a sort of karmic baggage. This is a bundle of emotions, developed largely through the experiences, from the time the customer sees the ad, to the time he goes to the distributor, buys the car, drives it, and then has a feeling of 'paisa vasool' (value for money). The degree of the 'paisa vasool' feeling is what makes a customer stick to a company. This can be seriously affected if the cross badged cars are not able to fit into the emotional connect due to the fact that the car was manufactured by another company. Like, a car without a 'mai baap". No lineage. No 'ownership' feeling. The purchase of another company's car from your regular company can still leave you with a feeling of 'ye kya ho raha hai' (what's going on). And no strategy can address this aspect. On paper, there might appear to be a mutual fit and benefit, but beyond the paper, there is a real world

## The Three Boxes – the way forward for Indian companies

The faculty meeting today (11 8 2016) at SPJIMR in which many of our colleagues presented their ideas on the books that they had read over the last two weeks was a revelation. The ideas from the world's leading thinkers on varied subjects were not only absorbed but also built upon to check out their applicability to SPJIMR. One group even admitted to internal differences of opinion after a thorough analysis. leading to three different interpretations. It was recalled that Mr. Gopalakrishnan, a Tata Sons Director, had observed 'disagree, without being disagreeable'.

Amongst the books debated upon, one was the Three Box Solution by Vijay Govindarajan. A word about Govindarajan. After the untimely demise of Dr. CK Prahlad, the Indian management thinker's community in the US was left with a big deficit. This has been ably filled and strengthened by

Dr. Vijay Govindarajan, a professor well known for innovation and strategy writings, practice and consulting. Just like CKP he has been in touch with Indian companies and has helped many of them to become 'world class' through adoption of the 'Three Box Solution', a methodology which he has developed over the last 30 + years. Many companies in the US, like GE, have benefitted from his wisdom and advise.

The Three Boxes book has somethings unique, ideas which have not been mentioned and applied in the way that Dr. G has done. There are many thinkers in the field of business strategy – Drucker, Igor Ansoff, Ram Charan, CK Prahlad, and others. There are many more in the field of organisational transformation – Kotter, Ratan Tata, S. Ramadorai, Dr. Jamshed Irani, B.Muthuraman, and others. All these thinkers and practitioners have used all the three boxes but they have not emphasised the Box B2 in the way that Dr. G has done. They also have not looked at scenarios where running the current business very well, and, at the same time, incubating new businesses which will lead their companies in new directions, in the way that Dr. G has written about.

Take, for example, the work done by Dr. Irani, the then MD of Tata Steel, in the year 1999 – 2000 in the incubation of the First eCommerce effort in India to sell steel and steel products. This was undertaken with full knowledge that five previous efforts in Germany and other developed countries had to close down. The running in and the successful commercialisation of Metal Junction – since rechristened as mjunction, and today the world's largest steel e-marketplace with a turnover exceeding Rs. 36,000 crores – while continuing to run Tata Steel at full efficiency at world class levels, is an excellent example of the B3 thinking. In order that B2 thinking should not hamper the new entity, a new MD was appointed and his office shifted out of Tata Steel, so that he could work without any interference from B1 and the foot dragging of B2.

The distinctive features of what Dr. G has written about is that B1 is for linear innovations, whereas B3 is for non-linear innovations. B3 is for experiments and B1 for certainties. The sooner the experiments are tested and found to be sound the better, a decision on whether to go ahead with the B3 idea should be made sooner than later. B1 and B3 need totally different hats and it is often not possible to run both at the same time. Metrics for B1 and B3 are quite different. B1 is next quarter, B3 is on the longer horizon. The secret is that B3 does not happen suddenly – the future is happening right now. According to Dr. G leaders in a company need to make the future happen every day, in small amounts, for which they need a set of competencies and skills which are not easily available in every company. Dr. G has cited several examples of how one can make B3 happen in M & A, in acquisitions, in ongoing companies like Hasbro, Keurit Coffee, the Protestant Church at Willow Creek, Illinois, TCS and the Mahindra Group.

The one distinguishing feature of Dr. G's version of running a company is the emphasis on B2. By linking this with Lord Shiva and the Trinity – Brahma, Vishnu and Mahesh - from the Hindu pantheon he has brought a perspective which is easy to understand and acceptable for implementation. Other philosophies also talk about this, but not in the same way. Jim

Collins, in his book on Good to Great talks about 'having the right people on the bus, and moving the wrong people out of it'. Lean management talks about 'moving out the 10% or so non-believers before undertaking lean changes'. Others have talked about 'unlearning' something before doing something new. However, the legitimacy of the scriptures that Dr. G has weighed in with is unique and provides an anchor. It is necessary to destroy parts of the old to ring in the new. If not, one is tempted to return to the old. Something akin to 'burning the bridge' after you cross it. You will never look back.

I think the book is an important contribution to the literature on how to run and manage companies in the long term and hopefully more groups in India will adopt this message.

## Lean Transformation and Indian Industry

If the words lean and transformation are put together to form 'Lean Transformation' the result is an intimidating scenario. While anorexia nervosa was in fashion many years back, and transformation is still being talked about and in use, lean transformation, LT for short, is neither intimidating nor about slimming. It is all about eliminating waste – and if that leads to a narrower waist, so be it.

When the term was used by Toyota to get out of the vicious 'low quality' (some spoke of Japanese quality of those days colourfully as 'yellow quality', sadly the Indian media was not present in those days to see it as another form of racism and rightly so) many people like Shoji Toyoda, Eichi Toyoda, Taichi Ohno (apocryphally speaking, it was said of Taichi that he was one of the toughest engineers to deal with, and people on the shop floors graced by him swear that, on seeing him near their machines, a collective 'Oh no, not him again' would go up,) were the founding fathers of the movement, one that would be the forerunner to Toyota becoming an exemplar of quality and lifetime joy for car owners.

This was way back in 1950. Since then, a lot of tsunamis have come and gone in Japan, but the power of LT has not subsided. If anything, it has become stronger and assumed titanicular proportions in the early 1990's when Womack and Jones came out with two books – Lean Thinking and the Machine that changed the world. Together with the film 'if Japan can, why can't we 'shown and seen by a million American managers in early 1980's, these books created a sense of tension in the American industry. After the books American industry relentlessly worked to adopt Japanese methods, including LT. The fear was that if they didn't, then they would have to report to Japanese bosses and learn Japanese as well to survive. There can be few things more motivating to a country brought up on the Flag and Apple Pie.

Within a few years the US industry leapfrogged and the Japanese were left behind. You may already be wondering, what was happening in India? As you might expect, as in all other things, based on the theme 'unity in diversity', a few Indian industry captains took interest in some aspects of lean but not the whole LT. Very few Indian industrialists were willing to go the whole hog. In fact, just getting into TQM itself was quite enervating and, huffing and puffing, a few industry giants and some pygmies as well (in the SSI's and MSME's) got into the act and crossed the first few milestones. No doubt even this effort paid rich dividends as many Indian companies shot into fame by getting into supply agreements with international giants – GM, Ford, BMW, Suzuki, to name but a few. Some of the more diligent ones got to winning the Deming Prize – Lucas TVS, Rane Madras, Sona Koyo Steering and lately Tata Steel - a coveted trophy of the highest honour in the world of quality manufacturing.

Over the years LT has become the norm in many companies all over the world. Like a rolling stone, since NO ONE could copy what Toyota has accomplished, despite the fact that Toyota invites everyone to come to its plants and see for themselves whatever they want to, no confidentiality, full transparency, LT has come to include many factors – TQM, customer intimacy, integrated industrial development, elimination of waste – so much so that many American companies got together to start and run successfully the Lean Advancement Initiative at the MIT (year 2000) which led to further embedment of LT in large corporates as well smaller ones. More companion initiatives like LESAT, Lean Enterprise Institutes and LT consultants have supported a broad-based movement to initiate LT. The latest developments in the world – climate change, environment conservation, elimination of toxic wastes, conservation, sustainability, CSR – have all worked in favour of the core concept of Lean – eliminate wastes in any form. In Japanese they call waste as 'muda'. In view of the many pressures (as in

Kyoto, Beijing, Dubai) many more companies are getting into the 'mooda' to eliminate waste and we should soon see the effects in India too.

www.ingramcontent.com/pod-product-compliance
Ingram Content Group UK Ltd.
Pitfield, Milton Keynes, MK11 3LW, UK
UKHW042018190726
13854UKWH00005B/2344